Learning to Think
Thinking to Learn

Models and Strategies
to Develop a Classroom Culture
of Thinking

Michael Pohl

Dedication

This book is dedicated to all those teachers who share my belief that the teaching of thinking is an empowering process that will see students of today become the critical, creative and caring adults of tomorrow who are capable of making the world a better place for everyone.

Acknowledgments

I wish to acknowledge the contributions made, both directly and indirectly, by the many teachers in South Australian schools with whom I have conferred over the creation of this publication. Without their input, support and encouragement, this book would not have been completed.

Some of the activities presented in this book are the product of collaborative planning sessions that I have facilitated during the past two years. I wish to thank all those teachers who have seeded the ideas, provided the inspiration and contributed to the activities in what I hope will be a valuable resource for teachers, schools and students alike.

I would also like to express my gratitude to my wife, Karen, for her continued support, suggestions, encouragement and proofreading skill.

©2000 Hawker Brownlow Education
Layout and cover design by Joanne Davis

All rights reserved
Printed and published in Australia

ISBN 1 74025 048 6
Code #4552

Contents

Foreword

This book is a practical guide for teachers at all levels of schooling as they plan and implement learning activities with a thinking focus. It describes processes that can be used to infuse thinking into everyday learning through the application and explicit teaching of various models and strategies. These strategies will see students engaging in a wide range of thinking tasks regardless of whether they are working within defined subject areas or on units that cut across traditional curriculum boundaries.

In a previous publication, I described a whole-school approach to the explicit teaching of thinking skills in the primary years. It was suggested there that a direct approach to teaching thinking was central to developing a thinking culture within a school.

The first chapter of this book builds on that publication and talks about what is meant by a 'culture of thinking'. More specifically, it describes what teachers can do to foster a classroom culture of thinking, and outlines how such a culture might affect student learning processes.

Subsequent chapters give specific examples of models and strategies most applicable at different levels of schooling. Both subject-specific and cross-curriculum examples are given for the primary, middle and upper levels.

Much of the book is devoted to practical examples of infused thinking.

The new revised Bloom's Taxonomy is introduced, Gardner's Multiple Intelligences as a planning tool is explored and the application of strategies such as Tony Ryan's Thinker's Keys are included. A range of other, lesser known models and strategies that encourage analytical, critical, creative and caring thinking are also described.

This equips teachers with a diverse range of tools that will assist in bringing about a culture of thinking in their classrooms and across their schools.

Introduction

The Role of Teachers in Creating a Culture of Thinking

As suggested in the foreword, creating a school-wide culture of thinking will require specific action on behalf of teachers and students alike. An essential element in developing a thinking culture will be the explicit teaching of thinking skills to all students.

Teachers will also be required to design teaching and learning activities that will:

engage students in a wide range of analytical, critical and creative thinking tasks.

create on-going opportunities for students to
- learn and expand their use of the language of thinking
- develop, practise and refine their thinking skills
- share their thinking in many ways and in all curriculum areas.

provide students with the tools to:
- manage
- organise
- record
. . . their thinking.

promote productive thinking, ie taking students beyond memorisation and simple recall into the higher order thinking skills of analysis, synthesis and evaluation.

assist in the transfer of skills as tools for life-long learning.

encourage students to apply thinking tools and strategies in everyday situations and in solving problems they encounter in the real world.

Clearly this will require both a whole-school approach to the explicit teaching of thinking skills and the ongoing application of an extensive range of models and thinking strategies by teachers as they create meaningful learning activities for students.

> An essential element in developing a thinking culture will be the explicit teaching of thinking skills to all students.

Teachers have an extensive range of models, strategies and tools available to assist them in infusing thinking into the curriculum. Some of these have gained wide acceptance and are used extensively. For example, there is any number of excellent resources for teachers that provide examples of how frameworks such as Bloom's Taxonomy of Cognitive Objectives or Gardner's Multiple Intelligences may be applied in the planning of learning activities for students. Indeed, the application of both models at all levels of schooling is show-cased in later chapters of this book.

However, whilst acknowledging the value of both frameworks, teachers will need to look 'beyond Bloom's as they establish a culture of thinking in their schools. Employing a range of frameworks in the planning of teaching and learning activities will assist teachers in maintaining student motivation and interest. In addition, employing some different instructional approaches in planning learning activities can be a refreshing and rewarding challenge for teachers who have relied on a narrow range of planning structures in the past.

A range of instructional approaches have been selected. Some of these will evoke specific types of thinking (eg. critical, creative and caring thinking).

Others will:
- cover a broad range of thinking skills
- allow for different ways of knowing and understanding
- focus specifically on the affective components of learning
- integrate models and strategies so as to encourage a range of thinking and feeling processes.

Employing a range of frameworks in the planning of teaching and learning activities will assist teachers in maintaining student motivation and interest.

Instructional Approaches to Develop a Broad Range of Thinking Skills and Processes

Using a variety of models in designing teaching and learning activities will encourage students to think in different ways as they work their way through specific activities.

This section introduces four different planning models that encourage students to employ a wide range of thinking skills and processes. Following the introduction to each model, practical examples are provided from different levels of schooling and from different areas of the curriculum.

The models to be discussed include
- The newly revised Bloom's Taxonomy
- Extended Brainstorming
- Tony Ryan's Thinker's Keys
- Directed Thinking

The Newly Revised Bloom's Taxonomy

The Taxonomy of Cognitive Objectives was first developed by Benjamin Bloom in the 1950s as a means of expressing qualitatively different kinds of thinking. Bloom's Taxonomy has since been adapted for classroom use as a planning tool and continues to be one of the most universally applied models across all levels of schooling and in all areas of study.

During the 1990s, Lorin Anderson (a former student of Benjamin Bloom) led a team of cognitive psychologists in revisiting the taxonomy with the view to examining the relevance of the taxonomy as we enter the twenty-first century.

Using a variety of models in designing, teaching and learning activities will encourage students to think in different ways.

Bloom's Taxonomy

Section One
Instructional
approaches to
develop a broad
range of thinking
skills and
processes.

As a result of the investigation a number of significant improvements were made to the existing structure. Before turning to examples of how the newly revised taxonomy may be applied, it would be appropriate at this point to make both the revisions and reasons for the changes explicit. Figure1 below describes both the 'old' and the 'new' taxonomies:

Bloom's Original Taxonomy		**Anderson's Revised Taxonomy**
Knowledge	➝	Remembering
Comprehension	➝	Understanding
Application	➝	Applying
Analysis	➝	Analysing
Synthesis	➝	Evaluating
Evaluation	➝	Creating

• Figure 1 – The original taxonomy and the revised taxonomy

Some of the more significant changes include changes in terminology, structure and emphasis. Summarising each in turn:

Changes in Terminology

1. As depicted in the previous table, the names of six major categories were changed from noun to verb forms. The reasoning behind this is that the taxonomy reflects different forms of thinking and thinking is an active process. Verbs, not nouns, describe actions, hence the change.

2. The subcategories of the six major categories were also replaced by verbs and some subcategories were reorganised.

3. The knowledge category was renamed. Knowledge is an outcome or product of thinking not a form of thinking per se. Consequently, the word knowledge was inappropriate to describe a category of thinking and was replaced with the word 'remembering'.

4. Comprehension and synthesis were retitled to 'understanding' and 'creating' respectively, in order to better reflect the nature of the thinking defined in each category.

Bloom's Taxonomy continues to be one of the most universally applied models across all levels of schooling and in all areas of study.

©2000 Hawker Brownlow Education #4552

The Taxonomy Table and The Knowledge Dimension

Type of Knowledge/ Cognitive Process	Factual	Conceptual	Procedural	Meta-cognitive
Remembering	▓			
Understanding		▓		
Applying			▓	
Analysing				▓
Evaluating				▓
Creating				▓

▓ By their nature and intent, certain question types tend to fall within certain (predictable) categories.

• Figure 2

Section One
Instructional
approaches to
develop a broad
range of thinking
skills and
processes.

Changes in Structure

1. The one-dimensional form of the original taxonomy becomes a two-dimensional table with the addition of the products of thinking (i.e. various forms of knowledge). Forms of knowledge are listed in the revised taxonomy as factual, conceptual, procedural and metacognitive. The relationship between the four knowledge types and the six levels of the taxonomy are explored in Figure 2.

2. The major categories were ordered in terms of increased complexity. As a result, the order of synthesis (create) and evaluation (evaluate) have been interchanged. This is in deference to the popularly held notion that if one considers the taxonomy as a hierarchy reflecting increasing complexity, then creative thinking (i.e creating level of the revised taxonomy) is a more complex form of thinking than critical thinking (i.e. evaluating level of the new taxonomy).

Put quite simply, one can be critical without being creative (i.e. judge an idea and justify choices) but creative production often requires critical thinking (i.e. accepting and rejecting ideas on the path to creating a new idea, product or way of looking at things.)

Changes in Emphasis

1. The revision's primary focus is on the taxonomy in use. Essentially, this means that the revised taxonomy is a more authentic tool for curriculum planning, instructional delivery, and some would argue, for assessment as well.

2. The revision is aimed at a broader audience. Bloom's Taxonomy was traditionally viewed as a tool best applied in the earlier years of schooling (i.e. primary and junior primary years). The revised taxonomy is more universal and easily applicable at primary, secondary and even tertiary levels.

3. The revision emphasises explanation and description of subcategories.

For example, sub-categories at the Remembering level of the taxonomy include:

Recognising/Identifying – Locating knowledge in memory that is consistent with presented material.

Recalling/Retrieving/Naming – Retrieving relevant knowledge from long-term memory.

Figure 3 gives a comprehensive overview of the sub-categories, along with some suggested question starters that aim to evoke thinking specific to each level of the taxonomy. Suggested potential activities and student products are also listed.

Examples of how the newly revised taxonomy may be applied appear on the pages that follow. These pages contain:

- two literary units of work designed for students working within the theme of fairy stories in their primary years of schooling.

- a unit of work designed for students working in the primary years of schooling in a thematic study of health and beauty.

- a unit of work designed for students working within the middle years of schooling on a theme of work and careers.

- a unit of work designed for students working within the later years of secondary schooling on a theme around Shakespeare's Macbeth.

- a blank planning proforma for teachers to use in developing their own units of work.

The revised taxonomy is a more authentic tool for curriculum planning, instructional delivery, and perhaps also for assessment.

Category	Sample sentence starters	Potential activities and products
Remembering *Recognising:* Locating knowledge in memory that is consistent with presented material. Synonyms: Identifying *Recalling:* Retrieving relevant knowledge from long-term memory. Synonyms: Retrieving/Naming	What happened after...? How many...? What is...? Who was it that...? Can you name ...? Find the meaning of... Describe what happened when... Who spoke to...? Which is true or false...? Identify who... Name all the......	Make a list of the main events of the story. Make a time line of events. Make a facts chart. Write a list of any pieces of information you can remember. What animals were in the story? Make a chart showing... Make an acrostic. Recite a poem.
Understanding *Interpreting:* Changing from one form of representation to another. Synonyms: Paraphrasing, Translating, Representing, Clarifying *Exemplifying:* Finding a specific example or illustration of a concept or principle. Synonyms: Instantiating, Illustrating *Classifying:* Determining that something belongs to a category (e.g., concept or principle). Synonyms: Categorising, Subsuming *Summarising:* Drawing a logical conclusion from presented information. Synonyms: Abstracting, Generalising *Inferring:* Abstracting a general theme or major point. Synonyms: Extrapolating, Interpolating, Predicting, Concluding *Comparing:* Detecting correspondences between two ideas, objects, etc. Synonyms: Contrasting, Matching, Mapping *Explaining:* Constructing a cause-and-effect model of a system. Synonyms: Constructing models	Can you write in your own words...? How would you explain...? Can you write a brief outline...? What do you think could have happened next? Who do you think...? What was the main idea? Clarify why – Illustrate the – Does everyone act in the way that .... does? Draw a story map Explain why a character acted in the way that they did.	Cut out, or draw pictures to show a particular event. Illustrate what you think the main idea may have been. Make a cartoon strip showing the sequence of events. Write and perform a play based on the story. Retell the story in your own words. Write a summary report of the event. Prepare a flow chart to illustrate the sequence of events. Make a colouring book.

Category	Sample sentence starters	Potential activities and products
Applying **Executing:** Applying knowledge (often procedural) to a routine task. Synonyms: Carrying out **Implementing:** Applying knowledge (often procedural) to a non-routine task. Synonyms: Using	Do you know of another instance where...? Can you group by characteristics such as...? Which factors would you change if...? What questions would you ask of...? From the information given, can you develop a set of instructions about...?	Construct a model to demonstrate how it works. Make a diorama to illustrate an event. Make a scrapbook about the areas of study. Make a papier-mache map/clay model to include relevant information about an event. Take a collection of photographs to demonstrate a particular point. Make up a puzzle game. Write a textbook about this topic for others.
Analysing **Differentiating:** Distinguishing relevant from irrelevant parts or important from unimportant parts of presented material. Synonyms: Discriminating, Selecting, Focusing, Distinguishing **Organising:** Determining how elements fit or function within a structure. Synonyms: Outlining, Structuring, Integrating, Finding coherence **Attributing:** Determining the point of view, bias, values, or intent underlying presented material. Synonyms: Deconstructing	Which events could not have happened? If – happened, what might the ending have been? How is – similar to – ? What do you see as other possible outcomes? Why did – changes occur? Can you explain what must have happened when...? What are some or the problems of...? Can you distinguish between...? What were some of the motives behind...? What was the turning point? What was the problem with...?	Design a questionnaire to gather information. Write a commercial to sell a new product. Make a flow chart to show the critical stages. Construct a graph to illustrate selected information. Make a family tree showing relationships. Devise a play about the study area. Write a biography of a person studied. Prepare a report about the area of study.

Category	Sample sentence starters	Potential activities and products
Evaluating **Checking:** Detecting inconsistencies or fallacies within a process or product. Determining whether a process or product has internal consistency. Synonyms: Testing, Detecting, Monitoring **Critiquing:** Detecting the appropriateness of a procedure for a given task or problem. Synonyms: Judging	Is there a better solution to…? Judge the value of – What do you think about…? Can you defend your position about…? Do you think – is a good or bad thing? How would you have handled…? What changes to – would you recommend? Do you believe – How would you feel if…? How effective are…?	Conduct a debate about an issue of special interest. Make a booklet about five rules you see as important. Convince others. Form a panel to discuss views. Write a letter to – advising on changes needed. Write a half-year report. Prepare a case to present your view about –
Creating **Generating:** Coming up with alternatives or hypotheses based on criteria. Synonyms: Hypothesising **Planning:** Devising a procedure for accomplishing a task. Synonyms: Designing, Producing **Producing:** Inventing a product. Synonyms: Constructing	Can you design a – to…? Can you see a possible solution to…? If you had access to all resources, how would you deal with…? Why don't you devise your own way to…? What would happen if…? How many ways can you…? Can you create new and unusual uses for…? Can you develop a proposal which would…?	Invent a machine to do a specific task. Design a building to house your study. Create a new product. Give it a name and plan a marketing campaign. Write about your feelings in relation to – Write a TV show, play, puppet show, role play, song or pantomime about – Design a record, book or magazine cover for – Sell an idea. Devise a way to –

• Figure 3: The revised taxonomy – Subcategories, question starters, activities and products

The Revised Taxonomy

Remembering

Recognise, list, describe, identify retrieve, name ...

Can the student **recall** information?

Understanding

Interpret, exemplify, summarise, infer, paraphrase ...

Can the student **explain** ideas or concepts?

Applying

Implement, carry out, use ...

Can the student **use** the new knowledge in another familiar situation?

Analysing

Compare, attribute, organise, deconstruct ...

Can the student **differentiate** between constituent parts?

Evaluating

Check, critique, judge hypothesise ...

Can the student **justify** a decision or course of action?

Creating

Design, construct, plan, produce ...

Can the student **generate** new products, ideas or ways of viewing things?

Planning Teaching and Learning Activities with a Thinking Skills Focus

Years P-6

Using Bloom's Taxonomy

Fairy Stories

Remembering *Factual answers, recall and recognition*	List all the fairy stories you have heard. Put a star next to those that start 'Once upon a time…'	Name some fairy story characters who are: mean, friendly, or members of a royal family.	Name some fairy stories in which animals play an important part.
Understanding *Translating, interpreting, showing understanding*	Think about a fairy story you know well. Is there an important message in the story?	Tell a favourite fairy story to a friend.	Make your own cartoon strip about a fairy story.
Applying *Using information gained in different, familiar situations*	Create a story map of a fairy story of your choice.	Make a model of a beanstalk using twigs, leaves and other natural materials.	Perform a favourite fairy story with a group of class members.
Analysing *Break into parts to examine more closely*	Select two fairy stories and find as many ways as you can to show how they are the same and how they are different.	Select a main character from a fairy story. Do an A-Z of words to describe what they are like.	Draw pictures of four important happenings in a story of your choice. Challenge a friend to put words to describe what they show.
Evaluating *Judge, use criteria, rank, substantiate*	Write a letter to the Big Bad Wolf saying what you think of him. Tell him why you think this way.	What would be the most difficult thing about living with a fire-breathing dragon?	What problems would you face if a giant came to live at your house?
Creating *Combine information with new situations to create new products, ideas, etc.*	Compose a song that Little Red Riding Hood might sing on the way to Grandma's house.	Invent a way to capture a giant without hurting him.	Design a carriage for Cinderella made from something other than a pumpkin.

Planning Teaching and Learning Activities with a Thinking Skills Focus

Using Bloom's Taxonomy

Years P-6

The Story of Hansel and Gretel

Remembering *Factual answers, recall and recognition*	List some reasons why Hansel and Gretel were left in the woods.	Describe the owner of the gingerbread house.	Name all the characters in the story.
Understanding *Translating, interpreting, showing understanding*	Explain why the witch lived in a gingerbread house.	Outline Gretel's oven plan.	Describe what happened the second time the children were left in the woods.
Applying *Using information gained in different, familiar situations*	Build a model of the witch's house.	Construct a story map of one journey into the woods.	Paint a scene from the story.
Analysing *Break into parts to examine more closely*	Differentiate between an event in the story you liked and one that you did not.	Examine the witch's thoughts as she fed Hansel and Gretel and present them to the class.	Think of another witch you have read about and compare her with the witch in this story.
Evaluating *Judge, use criteria, rank, substantiate*	Evaluate the father's actions. Was he a good father and a good husband?	Who you believe was the most clever character? Why?	Recall all the stepmothers you have read about. Rank them in order of most kind to most cruel.
Creating *Combine information with new situations to create new products, ideas, etc.*	Produce and present a plan to show how you would treat Hansel and Gretel.	Recreate the story with Hansel and Gretel finding an empty house in the forest.	Invent some other plans for finding your way home when you are lost pretending you are Hansel and Gretel.

Planning Teaching and Learning Activities with a Thinking Skills Focus
Using Bloom's Taxonomy

Health and Beauty (Collaborative group activity)   Years P-6

	Body Shape – Your Choice	Fitness and Exercise	You Are What You Eat	Drug Use and Abuse
Remembering *Factual answers, recall and recognition*	Display pictures of the human body collected from a range of different magazines.	What are some ways you might increase your level of fitness?	Tell about the role of the five major food groups in maintaining a healthy body.	Define the following: *drug abuse, addiction, rehabilitation.*
Understanding *Translating, interpreting, showing understanding*	Make a list of words often used to describe women. Do the same for men.	What are some benefits of regular exercise and a sensible diet?	Develop a set of rules for healthy eating.	Describe some of the symptoms or signs that may indicate that someone has a drug addiction.
Applying *Using information gained in different, familiar situations*	Prepare a description of a friend. Do not include a description of his/her physical appearance.	Use the information from above to make a picture book for young readers about the do's and don'ts of exercise.	Make up a puppet play using fruit and vegetable characters telling why they are good for the body.	Make a card game where players must match words to do with drugs and their meanings.
Analysing *Break into parts to examine more closely*	Use a Venn Diagram to depict the lists of male/female qualities you made earlier. Discuss findings in your group.	Prepare a matrix showing names of fitness centres in your area and the facilities available at each one.	Make a picture graph of foods you eat over one week. Comment on your graph.	What are possible long and short term advantages and disadvantages for athletes who chose to use performance enhancing drugs?
Evaluating *Judge, use criteria, rank, substantiate*	Write a strongly worded article supporting the view that advertising agencies should promote realistic body images for both sexes.	View some TV ads that feature fitness machines that promise to 'work miracles'. Do a P.M.I. for one such machine.	Select a range of foods available in the canteen. Rank them from most healthy to least healthy according to your own criteria.	Why do you think some people strongly object to the advertising of 'socially acceptable' drugs?
Creating *Combine information with new situations to create new products, ideas, etc.*	Design an advertisement for a magazine that features the qualities of a friend that you created earlier.	Using a range of suitable music tapes, create a 20 minute exercise workout suitable for your class group.	Make up a picnic basket full of interesting food that is both healthy and fun to eat.	Create a humorous cartoon strip that provides useful information about the dangers of drug abuse.

Planning Teaching and Learning Activities with a Thinking Skills Focus

Work and Careers

Years 7-9

	WHAT IS WORK?	TYPES OF WORK	STEREOTYPING	INFLUENCES
Remembering *Factual answers, recall and recognition*	Give 5 examples of different types of jobs. What is the difference between work and leisure?	List all the jobs you can think of in 10 minutes (individual or in groups).	What jobs are only available to one gender?	Interview 10 classmates and find out what type of work they would like to do.
Understanding *Translating, interpreting, showing understanding*	Suggest reasons why people have to work. What benefits do people obtain from working?	Why do certain jobs attract higher pay rates than others?	Give examples of occupations which use gender inclusive titles. Which occupations do not use such titles?	What are some of the influences on the choice of work?
Applying *Using information gained in different, familiar situations*	What are some jobs that can be done equally as well from home as from an office? How can this be achieved?	Decide how you could classify these occupations into different groups, eg. inside/outside; paid/unpaid, etc.	Examine the types of occupations portrayed by men and women in popular TV programs. Can any conclusions be drawn?	Discuss what makes a 'good job'. List some things that would improve your present working environment.
Analysing *Break into parts to examine more closely*	Contrast/Compare paid and unpaid work. What makes a successful career?	Classify the occupations, and publish and display your work using a graphic organiser.	Analyse the qualities of a person in a non-traditional occupation.	What influence has computer technology had on job choices?
Evaluating *Judge, use criteria, rank, substantiate*	Do you think people should be paid for all the work that they undertake? Give your reasons.	What kind of job would you like to have? List 5 things that interest you about this type of work.	How would you feel if you were denied the right to the career of your choice? Explain.	Investigate laws which help to protect workers. Why do you think these laws were created?
Creating *Combine information with new situations to create new products, ideas, etc.*	What would happen if all housework/child care became paid work?	Use SCAMPER to help you create a new occupation.	Compose a song to encourage someone to undertake a non-traditional occupation.	Design and/or construct a model of the perfect work environment.

©2000 Hawker Brownlow Education #4552

Planning Teaching and Learning Activities with a Thinking Skills Focus

Using Bloom's Taxonomy

Shakespeare's Macbeth

Years 10-12

Remembering *Factual answers, recall and recognition*	What were the three titles used by the witches in greeting Macbeth?	What prophecy did the witches have for Macbeth?	List the main characters in the story of Macbeth.
Understanding *Translating, interpreting, showing understanding*	What is a soliloquy? Give two examples from the play.	What evidence is there that perhaps the witches could foresee the future?	What do we learn about Lady Macbeth from the sleepwalking scene? (See Act V).
Applying *Using information gained in different, familiar situations*	Continue the speech by Macbeth and Banquo (after reading lines 38-88 Act I, Scene 3.)	Prepare invitations for the banquet including all relevant information.	Write a diary entry for Macbeth upon being crowned.
Analysing *Break into parts to examine more closely*	Compare and contrast Macbeth's and Banquo's reaction to the witches.	Draw a graph to illustrate the structure of the play.	How did Lady Macbeth contribute to her husband's downfall?
Evaluating *Judge, use criteria, rank, substantiate*	What can you infer about Lady Macbeth from her soliloquy? (Act I, Scene 5)	Give evidence from Act I that indicates the relationship between Macbeth and his wife.	Explain Malcolm's change of attitude toward Macbeth.
Creating *Combine information with new situations to create new products, ideas, etc.*	Compose a reply by Lady Macbeth to the letter she received in Act I.	Recreate the story - this time in a modern day setting and everyday language.	In groups, present a scene of your choice to the rest of the class.

Additional column (second activity column):

Remembering	Why does Macbeth fear Banquo? (See Act III, Scene 1)
Understanding	Why do you think Lady Macbeth wishes her husband to return home quickly? (Act I, Sc.5)
Applying	Draw an illustration of a scene that has captured your imagination.
Analysing	How did the witches contribute to Macbeth's downfall?
Evaluating	Give reasons for your impressions of Lady Macbeth up to Act II.
Creating	Create some other descriptive phrases that could be used instead of 'full of scorpions'. (Act V)

Planning Teaching and Learning Activities with a Thinking Skills Focus
Using Bloom's Taxonomy

Topic: _____

Year(s)-

Remembering *Factual answers, recall and recognition*			
Understanding *Translating, interpreting, showing understanding*			
Applying *Using information gained in different, familiar situations*			
Analysing *Break into parts to examine more closely*			
Evaluating *Judge, use criteria, rank, substantiate*			
Creating *Combine information with new situations to create new products, ideas, etc.*			

Section One
Instructional
approaches to
develop a broad
range of thinking
skills and
processes.

Extended Brainstorming

When asked whether they employ the brainstorming technique in their everyday teaching, teachers commonly reply by suggesting that they often ask students to generate lists of things for discussion. When asked what else they do besides generating lists (i.e. brainstorming for fluency), they generally are at a loss to respond.

Teaching Thinking in the Primary Years (Pohl, 1997) elaborates upon four cognitive components of brainstorming that will evoke different forms of thinking. These four cognitive components of brainstorming include:

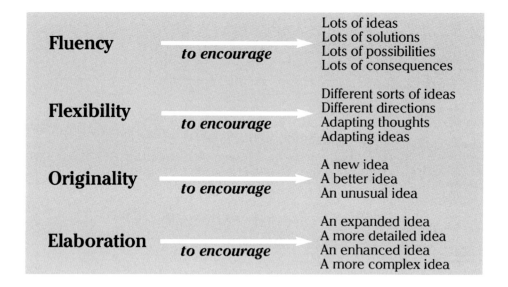

Fluency *to encourage*
Lots of ideas
Lots of solutions
Lots of possibilities
Lots of consequences

Flexibility *to encourage*
Different sorts of ideas
Different directions
Adapting thoughts
Adapting ideas

Originality *to encourage*
A new idea
A better idea
An unusual idea

Elaboration *to encourage*
An expanded idea
A more detailed idea
An enhanced idea
A more complex idea

Extended Brainstorming encourages students to develop both cognitive and affective components of thinking.

It is important to realise, however, that the teaching of these cognitive aspects of the brainstorming process can be extended to include an additional four elements with an affective focus.

Planning and programming with the four affective components of brainstorming in mind will see teachers encouraging:

Curiosity	*with questions like*	Suppose that What if? When might? Where could?
Complexity	*with questions like*	What reason could there be? What contributes to? What makes people? What factors contribute to?
Risk Taking	*with questions like*	Say why you think Justify why Which is better? Decide and explain
Imagination	*with questions like*	How would you feel if? Pretend that Imagine yourself in Think of a time when

Including these extra components provides teachers with a framework for developing a range of activities with a balance of both cognitive and affective outcomes.

Examples of how Extended Brainstorming may be applied to include all eight components appear on the pages that follow. These pages contain:

- a unit of work on minibeasts designed for students working within the primary years of schooling

- a unit of work on leisure designed for students working in the middle years of schooling

- a unit of work within a theme of the future designed for students working in the later years of their secondary schooling

- a blank proforma for teachers to use in developing their own units of work.

> **Including these extra components provides teachers with a framework for developing a range of activities with a balance of both cognitive and affective outcomes.**

Extended Brainstorming
Mini-Beasts
Years P-6

To encourage

Fluency	Flexibility	Originality	Elaboration	Curiosity	Complexity	Risk Taking	Imagination
Ask how many - ideas - solutions - possibilities - consequences	Ask how many *different* - kinds of ideas - categories of ideas - types of solutions - directions or pathways	Ask for - new or original ideas - better ideas - unusual ideas	Ask for - expanded ideas - detailed ideas - a plan of action - a complex idea	Ask questions that begin - Suppose that - What if? - When might? - Where could?	Ask questions that begin - What reason could there be? - What contributes to? - What makes people? - What factors contribute to?	Ask questions that begin - Say why you think - Justify why - Which is better? - Decide and explain	Ask questions that begin - How would you feel if? - Pretend that - Imagine yourself in
List: - all the mini-beasts you know - ways mini-beasts protect themselves - places to find mini-beasts - all the facts you know about mini-beasts	How many different ways can you group mini-beasts?	You have just discovered a new mini-beast that has never before been seen. Describe what it looks like, where you found it and anything special about it.	A spider is a mini-beast, but is it an insect? What do you think? Tell how you would convince someone that your explanation is correct.	If you were to interview an ant, a butterfly, a bee or some other mini-beasts, what questions would you ask?	What makes people want to kill insects? Why do you think that insects are not found in oceans? What makes a mini-beasts useful?	Explain why you think it might be better to be - a butterfly or a moth - a wasp or a bee - an ant or a cockroach	You are a flea living on a dog. Tell about your life and adventures. What if flies were the size of cats? What would it be like to change from a caterpillar into a butterfly?

©2000 Hawker Brownlow Education #4552

Extended Brainstorming
Vacation Time!

Years 7-9

To encourage

Fluency	Flexibility	Originality	Elaboration	Curiosity	Complexity	Risk Taking	Imagination
Ask how many - ideas - solutions - possibilities - consequences	Ask how many **different** - kinds of ideas - categories of ideas - types of solutions - directions or pathways	Ask for - new or original ideas - better ideas - unusual ideas	Ask for - expanded ideas - detailed ideas - a plan of action - a complex idea	Ask questions that begin - Suppose that - What if? - When might? - Where could?	Ask questions that begin - What reason could there be? - What contributes to? - What makes people? - What factors contribute to?	Ask questions that begin - Say why you think - Justify why - Which is better? - Decide and explain	Ask questions that begin - How would you feel if? - Pretend that - Imagine yourself in
List: - holiday activities that are inexpensive - activities that you know your parents would enjoy doing with you - activities you would offer at a holiday camp for kids of your own age	What are all the things you would need to think about if you were planning an interstate holiday?	Draw a timeline depicting your ideal holiday in a make-believe location.	Prepare a detailed one-week itinerary for an interstate holiday. Take into account all the things you thought were important planning considerations.	How would life be different for you if you went to school at night and stayed at home during the day?	What makes Australia a popular destination for overseas visitors?	Imagine the plane you were in was forced to land in the desert and you were the only one fit enough to look for help. How might you survive alone in the desert on your trek to gain help?	You have been asked to create a new national holiday. What will you choose to celebrate? Explain your choice.

Extended Brainstorming
The Future

Years 10-12

To encourage

Fluency	Flexibility	Originality	Elaboration	Curiosity	Complexity	Risk Taking	Imagination
Ask how many - ideas - solutions - possibilities - consequences	*Ask how many* ***different*** - kinds of ideas - categories of ideas - types of solutions - directions or pathways	*Ask for* - new or original ideas - better ideas - unusual ideas	*Ask for* - expanded ideas - detailed ideas - a plan of action - a complex idea	*Ask questions that begin* - Suppose that - What if? - When might? - Where could?	*Ask questions that begin* - What reason could there be? - What contributes to? - What makes people? - What factors contribute to?	*Ask questions that begin* - Say why you think - Justify why - Which is better? - Decide and explain	*Ask questions that begin* - How would you feel if? - Pretend that - Imagine yourself in
List: - ways to overcome food shortages - possible ways to ensure survival of endangered animals	What do you see as the 'top ten' issues for the world in the next twenty years?	Create the lyrics for a song about the destruction of native flora in a region of your choice. Include a message of hope.	You are to host a meeting of world leaders and you are asked to prepare an agenda for that meeting. What will you include? How will you decide on the priority of the agenda items?	Suppose you were allowed to create a new law that gave teenagers a right they do not currently have under law. What might be some positive and negative consequences?	What effect has computer technology had on our everyday lives? How might we further apply this technology to make the future a better place for lesser-developed countries?	Which will be more important for the future – education, equality or harmony? Justify your choice.	Create a recipe for world peace. What are the main ingredients? How are they meant to be blended together?

Extended Brainstorming

Year(s)-

Topic: _____

Fluency	Flexibility	Originality	Elaboration	Curiosity	Complexity	Risk Taking	Imagination
			To encourage				
Ask how many - ideas - solutions - possibilities - consequences	Ask how many *different* - kinds of ideas - categories of ideas - types of solutions - directions or pathways	Ask for - new or original ideas - better ideas - unusual ideas	Ask for - expanded ideas - detailed ideas - a plan of action - a complex idea	Ask questions that begin - Suppose that - What if? - When might? - Where could?	Ask questions that begin - What reason could there be? - What contributes to? - What makes people? - What factors contribute to?	Ask questions that begin - Say why you think - Justify why - Which is better? - Decide and explain	Ask questions that begin - How would you feel if? - Pretend that - Imagine yourself in

Thinker's Keys

Teaching Thinking in the Primary Years (Pohl 1997) elaborates upon eight Thinker's Keys for explicit instruction. First developed by Tony Ryan, (*Thinker's Keys for Kids*, 1990) Thinker's Keys were a set of twenty different activities designed to motivate and engage students in a wide range of thinking tasks.

A range of question starters are presented as keys to unlocking the analytical, critical and creative thinking abilities of students.

A summary of the twenty keys appears below.

The Reverse	Places words such as 'cannot', 'never' and 'would not' in sentences which are commonly displayed in a listing format. e.g. List things you would never see in Australia.
The What If	You can ask virtually any *What if* question (serious or frivolous). Students record thinking on a graphic organiser.
The Alphabet	Students compile a list of words from A to Z which have some relevance to a given category which features in the area of study.
The Bar	The acronym - BAR can be used to improve on the design of everyday objects. B = Bigger A = Add R = Remove or Replace
The Construction	A problem solving task that requires the creative use of limited quantities of everyday materials
The Disadvantages	Here, students choose an object or a practice, and list a number of its disadvantages. Then they list some ways of connecting or eliminating these disadvantages.
Different Uses	Students put their imaginations to work as they list some widely different uses for a chosen object from an area of study.

• Adapted from Ryan T. (1990) *Thinker's Keys for Kids*. Woodridge, Qld: Logan West School Support Centre

The Prediction	Students think critically as they predict possible outcomes to a set of given circumstances or a particular situation.
The Picture	A simple diagram which has no relevance to the area of study is presented and the students then try to work out ways in which it could be linked with that area of study.
The Ridiculous	Make a ridiculous statement that would be virtually impossible to implement and then have students attempt to substantiate it.
The Commonality	Select two objects with little to do with each other and ask students to find points of commonality.
The Inventions	Students are encouraged to develop inventions which are constructed in an unusual manner or using unusual materials.
The Alternatives	Students list ways in which to complete a task without using the normal tools or implements.
The Question	Start with the answer, and try to list 5 questions which could be linked with that answer only.
The Brainstorming	State a problem which needs to be solved and have students brainstorm a list of solutions.
Forced Relationship	Students develop a solution to a problem by considering the attributes of a number of dissimilar objects.
The Combination	Students list the attributes of two unmatched objects, then combine the attributes to create a new or better product.
Interpretation	Describe an unusual situation and then ask students to think of some different explanations for the existence of that situation.
The Brick Wall	Make a statement which could not generally be questioned or disputed, and then try to break down the wall by finding other ways of dealing with the situation.
The Variations	Students find many ways to overcome an obstacle or solve a problem.

Thinker's Keys Question starters to unlock the analytical, critical and creative thinking abilities of students

Section One
Instructional
approaches to
develop a broad
range of thinking
skills and
processes.

Examples of Thinker's Keys activities that may be used within curriculum areas or within themes appear on the pages that follow. These pages contain:

- motivational activities designed for students engaged in a study of the Olympic Games

- motivational activities designed for students engaged in a study of Greek influences in Australia within a unit of work in Languages Other Than English (LOTE)

- motivational activities designed for students engaged in a study of occupations

- motivational activities designed for students engaged in a geographic study of our world

- an example of how Thinker's Keys may be used to create some interesting and unusual spelling and word knowledge activities

- a blank planning proforma for teachers to use in developing their own units of work.

Levels of schooling for these activities have not been identified. Whilst it may be most appropriate, for example, to use the activities described in the unit of work on occupations in the middle years of schooling, this should not preclude teachers at other levels of schooling from modifying and applying them at their level.

By their very nature, Thinker's Keys activities are easily adapted for use at most levels of schooling.

Thinker's Keys

Olympic Games

Area of Study/Theme/Topic

The Reverse	The What If?	The Disadvantages	The Combination	The Alphabet
Name 10 things you would *never* see at the Olympic Games.	What would be some possible consequences should the Commonwealth Games become more popular than the Olympic Games?	What are some disadvantages of the marathon being run over such a long distance? Suggest some solutions to the problems.	List and then combine some of the attributes of a javelin and a TV camera.	List words associated with the Olympic Games – A–Z.
The Bar	The Variations	The Picture	The Prediction	The Different Uses
Use BAR to improve the design or use of a piece of sporting equipment.	Suggest many ways that the host countries could be selected.	What could this picture have to do with the Olympic Games?	Suggest a sport that may be in the Olympic Games 50 years from now.	Find 10 different uses for a discarded hockey stick.
The Ridiculous	The Commonality	The Question	The Brainstorming	The Inventions
Try to justify this statement: No athletes should be sponsored by governments or commercial enterprise.	What are the commonalities between a spectator and a top athlete?	The answer is an Olympic Games medal. What are 5 possible questions?	Brainstorm solutions to some of the problems for the host country due to the expense of holding the Olympic Games.	Invent a new training regime for a top athlete.
The Interpretation	The Brick Wall	The Construction	The Forced Relationship	The Alternative
Give some possible reasons for a sudden change of venue for the games.	Consider some alternatives to the fact that many sports people will never compete in the Games.	Construct a winner's medal dais from egg cartons and sticky tape.	How might a long jumper use some or all of the following to leap 10 metres – a book, some straws, a radio and a bottle?	List some ways that you may attend the games without actually buying a ticket.

©2000 Hawker Brownlow Education #4552

Thinker's Keys

Greek Influences

Area of Study/Theme/Topic

The Reverse Name 10 places you would not find Greek migrants in Australia. What wouldn't you put in a yiros?	**The What If?** ...... we did not have Greek migrants in Australia? ... we all spoke Greek at school?	**The Disadvantages** List disadvantages and improvements to ......a Greek Festival.
The Combination List and then combine some of the attributes of a meat pie and a traditional Greek dish.	**The Alphabet** List A-Z words associated with Greece or the Greek language.	
The Bar Use BAR to improve the design or use of: 1. Greek coffee or 2. The Acropolis	**The Variations** Suggest many ways to say "hello", "goodbye", and "how are you?" in Greek.	**The Picture** What could this picture have to do with the Greek alphabet?
The Prediction Suggest how things may be different if Greeks all settled only in one part of Australia.	**The Different Uses** Find 10 different uses for: - worry beads - Yiros	
The Ridiculous Try to justify this statement: Everyone should learn about Greek culture and speak Greek.	**The Commonality** What are the commonalities between a shoelace and Greek dancing?	**The Question** The answer is Athens. What are 5 possible questions?
The Brainstorming Brainstorm ways to encourage Australians to visit Greece.	**The Inventions** Design a new Greek recipe.	
The Interpretation Give some possible reasons why someone might want to prevent Greeks from coming to Australia.	**The Brick Wall** Every school must teach another language. What alternatives are there?	**The Construction** Construct a close replica of the Acropolis using 1m. sticky tape, 20 straws and 1 A3 piece of cardboard.
The Forced Relationship How might the government use some or all of the following to encourage Greek migration - a book, paper clips and radio?	**The Alternative** List some ways that you may learn Greek without a teacher to help you.	

Thinker's Keys

Area of Study/Theme/Topic

Occupations

The Reverse	The What If?	The Disadvantages	The Combination	The Alphabet
Name 10 things you would never see on a farm.	What would be some possible consequences should all shops be able to choose when to open and when to close?	What are some disadvantages of having factories situated close to homes? Suggest some solutions to the problems.	List and then combine some of the attributes of windmills and a fire truck in order to improve the design of either one.	List A-Z words associated with occupations.
The Bar	The Variations	The Picture	The Prediction	The Different Uses
Use BAR to improve the design or use of a tractor.	Suggest many ways that different products are marketed and sold.	What could this picture have to do with getting a job?	Suggest some occupations that may exist 50 years from now and some that may not.	Find 10 different uses for an old factory.
The Ridiculous	The Commonality	The Question	The Brainstorming	The Inventions
Try to justify this statement: No-one should have to work more than two hours each day.	What are the commonalties between a plumber and a pilot?	The answer is hard work. What are 5 possible questions?	Brainstorm solutions to some of the problems faced by someone starting up their own business.	Design a robot that can do a job that most people do not want to do.
The Interpretation	The Brick Wall	The Construction	The Forced Relationship	The Alternative
Give some possible reasons why someone suddenly quit his/her job forever.	What are some things people who find it difficult to get a job might do to improve their chances?	Construct a bridge using 1m. sticky tape, 20 straws and 1 A4 piece of cardboard.	How might the police use some or all of the following to catch a thief - a book, paper clips, a radio and a bottle?	List some ways that you may earn money (legally) without actually going to work.

Thinker's Keys

Area of Study/Theme/Topic

The World Around Us

The Reverse	The What If?	The Disadvantages	The Combination	The Alphabet
List things you would never see in an atlas.	What if the world's population doubled within the next five years?	What are some disadvantages of an atlas? How might they be overcome?	List the attributes of rivers. Use these ideas to improve the design of freeways.	Do an A-Z of countries of the world.
The Bar	The Variations	The Picture	The Prediction	The Different Uses
Use the BAR key to improve a landform of your choosing.	How many ways can you cross the Atlantic?	What connections has this picture to an Atlas ?	What would be the consequences if most people lived in Central Australia?	List many uses for an out-of-date atlas.
The Ridiculous	The Commonality	The Question	The Brainstorming	The Inventions
What would happen if we all had to live underwater?	What do great mountain ranges and oranges have in common?	The answer is a compass. What are 5 questions that could have this answer?	Brainstorm ways to encourage tourism within Australia.	Invent a way of remembering the major capital cities of the world.
The Interpretation	The Brick Wall	The Construction	The Forced Relationship	The Alternative
The great pyramids are to be moved to London. Explain why this is so.	Consider alternatives to high density living.	How could you cross the Ganges River using a tennis ball, a rope and a brick?	How might an explorer use a pencil to find his way through thick jungle?	List ways to see the Leaning Tower of Pisa without actually going there.

Using Thinker's Keys to Develop Word Knowledge Activities

The Reverse
Choose a list word and use it to write a *reverse key*. (*For example*, Name 10 things you could never do underground.)

The What If?
Select a word and use it in a *What If* question. (*For example*, What if fuel prices doubled tomorrow?)

The Disadvantages
Choose a noun from your list and write all the disadvantages that you can find. Then suggest improvements for each one.

The Bar
Choose a noun from your list and use BAR to improve the design or use of the object.

The Alphabet
Take a theme word and compile a list of words from A-Z that link to the theme.

The Picture
Draw or find a shape of anything at all. Find as many links as you can between a list word and the picture.

The Combination
Combine the attributes of two list words to create a new or improved idea or invention.

The Commonality
Find 2 words in your list that at first thought have little in common. Now find as many shared properties for them as you can.

The Question
Choose a list word and write 5 questions that could only have this word as the answer.

Thinker's Keys

Area of Study/Theme/Topic

The **A**lphabet	The Different Uses	The Inventions	The Alternative
The Combination	The Prediction	The Brainstorming	The Forced Relationship
The Disadvantages	The Picture	The Question	The Construction
The What If?	The Variations	The Commonality	The Brick Wall
The Reverse	The Bar	The Ridiculous	The Interpretation

Directed Thinking

Section One
Instructional
approaches to
develop a broad
range of thinking
skills and
processes.

Why NO? Why WAIT? What ELSE? Way to GO!

Similar to Edward DeBono's Six Thinking Hats, Directed Thinking
encourages students to focus upon specific elements of an idea at
any given time. In this way, students avoid making hasty decisions or
rushing into something without giving due consideration to factors
that may otherwise have been overlooked. Judgement is deferred
until the full worth of ideas has been contemplated.

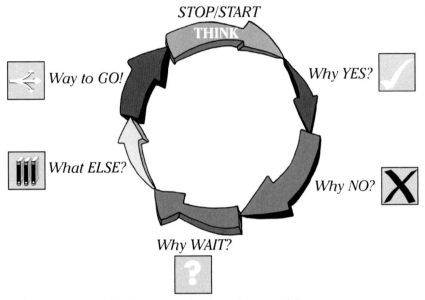

Students are required to devote time to consider:

- *Why YES?* - What are the good points about an idea, regardless of
  how they may feel about it?

- *Why NO?* - What are the negative aspects of the idea, regardless of
  how they may feel about it?

- *Why WAIT?* - What other alternatives and possibilities may be
  discovered?

- *What ELSE?* - What other information might they need to know
  before judging an idea?

- *Way to GO!* - Identify ways to implement a chosen idea or course
  of action after due consideration.

**With Directed
Thinking,
judgement is
deferred until
the full worth
of ideas
has been
contemplated.**

**Directed
Thinking**

**Students are
also
encouraged to
express how
they feel (or
how feelings
may have
changed) as a
result of the
directed
thinking
process.**

During the Directed Thinking process, students are also encouraged to express how they feel (or how feelings may have changed as a result of the directed thinking process) about particular ideas or actions, as an important part of the strategy.

Examples of how Directed Thinking may be applied appear on the pages that follow. These pages contain:

- a unit of work designed for primary students engaged in a study about themselves and their feelings.

- a unit of work designed for primary students engaged in a study of inventions.

- two units of work designed for students involved in Media Study – one topic investigates magazine covers and the other topic looks at video clips. These units are best introduced during the middle years of schooling.

- a proforma easily adapted for all levels of schooling for students evaluating a self-directed design task in technology.

- a proforma easily adapted for all levels of schooling for students as they respond to a shared novel or some individual reading.

- a blank planning proforma for teachers to use in developing their own units of work.

Years P-6

Directed Thinking Strategy
Theme: Me and My Feelings

Why Yes?	What are the good points about an idea, regardless of how you may feel about it?	Do an ABC of words that describe good things about you. A - adorable B - blushing C - cuddly … Finish this in as many ways as you can. Draw pictures for some of your answers – *Happiness is –*
Why No?	What are the negative aspects of the idea, regardless of how you may feel about it?	Mime someone doing something that makes them cross or angry. See if others can guess what you are doing. Draw the face of an angry person - how do you know that they are angry?
Why Wait?	What other alternatives and possibilities are there to be discovered?	How would you make someone feel better if they were upset? If food were feelings, then an apple would be – because – Do the same for other foods. How would you change the way you look if you could change just one thing?
What Else?	What other information might be needed before we judge an idea?	Record measurements of the different parts of your body on the class name chart. What is something that makes you special (unique) in your own way?
Way to Go!	How might you implement your chosen idea or course of action?	Think about how you change from being sad to being happy. Share some of these ways with a group of friends. Why do you think that you sometimes laugh at things that are not really funny? (Some cartoons, for example, show characters being hurt - and yet we laugh at them.)

Directed Thinking Strategy
Theme: Inventions

Years P-6

Why Yes?	What are the good points about an idea, regardless of how you may feel about it?	What are some of the advantages of an electric pencil sharpener over a hand held pencil sharpener? Try to think of at least five advantages.
Why No?	What are the negative aspects of the idea, regardless of how you may feel about it?	What are the disadvantages of television? Prepare a talk aimed at convincing others that all TVs should be banned.
Why Wait?	What other alternatives and possibilities are there to be discovered?	How might you use a clock, a straw and a paper bag to catch a mouse? Construct a model of a machine designed to wake you up in the morning. Invent a name for it and design an advertising poster for it.
What Else?	What other information might be needed before we judge an idea?	List inventions that you know for each letter of the alphabet. Collect pictures of machines and group them into categories of your own choosing.
Way to Go!	How might you implement your chosen idea or course of action?	You have two great ideas for new inventions — a better hair dryer and a better bicycle, but you only have enough time and money to create one of them. Which one would you select? Why? What steps would you take in making and marketing it?

Directed Thinking Strategy

Years 7-9

Theme: Media   Topic: **Magazine Covers**

Why Yes?	What are the good points about an idea, regardless of how you may feel about it?	Examine the cover of a magazine designed to appeal to your age group. What is pleasing about the presentation? Think about use of colour, layout, use of pictures, captions, clarity, etc.
Why No?	What are the negative aspects of the idea, regardless of how you may feel about it?	Are the images projecting any bias or stereotyping? What messages are being implied by some of the photographs or captions? Consider body image or the way one should look or act.
Why Wait?	What other alternatives and possibilities are there to be discovered?	How might the cover design be improved? Consider: 1. the use of techniques such as font styles, coloured type, underlining, etc. 2. visual aspects such as the use of colour pictures, cartoons, 3D effects, etc.
What Else?	What other information might be needed before we judge an idea?	Does the cover indicate the purpose of the magazine? Is it mainly to inform or entertain? What makes you think so? Do the articles highlighted on the cover live up to expectations?
Way to Go!	How might you implement your chosen idea or course of action?	How might you evaluate the effectiveness of a magazine cover? What criteria would you see as important? How does the cover of this magazine rate according to your criteria?

Directed Thinking Strategy

Years 7-9

Theme: **Media** *Topic:* **Viewing a Music Video**

Why Yes?	What are the good points about an idea, regardless of how you may feel about it?	List some of the good points about the video clip. Consider things like special effects, video/audio matching, editing, innovations, music and lyrics.
Why No?	What are the negative aspects of the idea, regardless of how you may feel about it?	Discuss ways in which the content of the video may not be suitable for particular age groups. Are there any stereotypical views about society's values being given directly or indirectly in this clip?
Why Wait?	What other alternatives and possibilities are there to be discovered?	Discuss ways in which the video clip may have been improved in its visual presentation, the music or the way in which it was presented. Design a new CD cover that draws upon the location or events depicted in the clip.
What Else?	What other information might be needed before we judge an idea?	What issues are being raised in the video clip? What prior knowledge may you need to have about the places, people or events depicted in the clip to fully appreciate it?
Way to Go!	How might you implement your chosen idea or course of action?	How important is editing in making a good video clip? Establish criteria for judging the quality of a video clip. How does this one 'measure up'?

All Year Levels

Directed Thinking Strategy

Theme: **Student Self Evaluation**   *Topic:* **Design Task**

Why Yes?	What are the good points about an idea, regardless of how you may feel about it?	List the good points of the design task set for you.
Why No?	What are the negative aspects of the idea, regardless of how you may feel about it?	What were some of the problems you encountered during this exercise?
Why Wait?	What other alternatives and possibilities are there to be discovered?	Describe some creative ways you overcame the difficulties you just described.
What Else?	What other information might be needed before we judge an idea?	Describe the task set for you in your own words.
Way to Go!	How might you implement your chosen idea or course of action?	What did you think about the task a whole? Which aspects of the task were frustrating? interesting? challenging? In what ways do you think that completing this task has been a valuable learning experience?

Directed Thinking Strategy

All Year Levels

Theme: **Novel Study** *Topic:* **Responding to a Text**

Why Yes?	What are the good points about an idea, regardless of how you may feel about it?	What were some of the more interesting, thought provoking parts of the story? What positive aspects of the story would you highlight?
Why No?	What are the negative aspects of the idea, regardless of how you may feel about it?	What were some of the problems encountered by the main character? How and why did they occur?
Why Wait?	What other alternatives and possibilities are there to be discovered?	In what ways were some of the problems or difficulties overcome? What other solutions were possible?
What Else?	What other information might be needed before we judge an idea?	What is the central theme of the novel? Describe characters, setting, plot.
Way to Go!	How might you implement your chosen idea or course of action?	In what ways do you think that reading this novel has contributed to your understanding of others? If you had written the novel, what might you have done differently?

Directed Thinking Strategy

Year(s)-

Theme: _____

Why Yes?	What are the good points about an idea, regardless of how you may feel about it?	
Why No?	What are the negative aspects of the idea, regardless of how you may feel about it?	
Why Wait?	What other alternatives and possibilities are there to be discovered?	
What Else?	What other information might be needed before we judge an idea?	
Way to Go!	How might you implement your chosen idea or course of action?	

Section
Two

Instructional Approaches to tap into Different Ways of Knowing and Understanding the World

Using a variety of models in designing teaching and learning activities will not only encourage students to think in different ways as suggested in the previous section, but may also provide them with diverse opportunities to demonstrate ways of knowing and understanding.

Planning units of work using Howard Gardner's Multiple Intelligences as a framework will allow students to experiment with a range of products to indicate content mastery.

This section introduces Multiple Intelligences as a versatile planning tool for teachers at all levels of schooling. Following the introduction, practical examples are provided from the primary level, the middle years of schooling and from different areas of the curriculum.

> **M.I. provides students with diverse opportunities to demonstrate ways of knowing and understanding.**

Gardner's Multiple Intelligences

Section 2
Instructional
approaches to
tap into different
ways of knowing
and
understanding
the world.

Howard Gardner's views on the nature of intelligence appeared in his 1983 publication, *Frames of Minds*. There he discussed the existence of not one single intelligence but rather the existence of many, culturally defined intelligences that work within the mind as the brain strives to better know and understand the world.

The theory of Multiple Intelligences (MI) initially described the range of discrete intelligences that could easily be identified. These intelligences included the:

- Verbal/Linguistic

- Music/Rhythmical

- Logical/Mathematical

- Intrapersonal

- Interpersonal

- Visual/Spatial

- Bodily/Kinaesthetic

- Naturalist*

Like Bloom's Taxonomy, Gardner's Multiple Intelligences are easily adaptable for classroom use as a planning tool and this model is quickly catching up to Bloom's as the most frequently applied model across all levels of schooling and in all areas of study.

**MI provides an
excellent
framework for
authentic
instruction and
assessment.**

MI provides an excellent framework for authentic instruction and assessment. As Figure 4 shows, a multiple intelligence approach to planning allows for the integration of content, skills development and a range of ways for students to demonstrate their learning beyond what has been traditionally offered.

On the next page is a brief summary of the preferred ways of knowing and understanding the world that may be demonstrated by students as they tap into different intelligence strengths.

* In 1995, the Naturalist Intelligence was added to seven previously identified intelligences. There is no reason to assume that these eight now form a definitive list of all possible forms of intelligence. Howard Gardner himself alludes to the existence of at least one more intelligence.

Gardner's Multiple Intelligences

Verbal/ Linguistic Learners	Like to –	Read. Write. Tell stories.
	Are good at –	Memorising names, places, dates and trivia.
	Learn best by –	Saying, hearing and seeing words.
Logical/ Mathematical Learners	Like to –	Do experiments. Figure things out. Work with numbers. Question.
	Are good at –	Categorising. Reasoning. Logic. Problem solving.
	Learn best by –	Classifying. Working with abstract patterns/relationships.
Visual/ Spatial Learners	Like to –	View pictures/slides. Watch movies. Play with machines.
	Are good at –	Imagining things. Sensing changes. Mazes/puzzles. Reading maps/charts.
	Learn best by –	Visualising. Dreaming. Using the mind's eye.
Musical Learners	Like to –	Sing/hum/listen to tunes. Play an instrument. Respond to music.
	Are good at –	Picking up sounds. Remembering melodies. Noticing pitches/rhythms. Keeping time.
	Learn best by –	Rhythm. Melody. Music.
Bodily/ Kinaesthetic Learners	Like to –	Move around. Touch and talk. Use body language.
	Are good at –	Physical activities (sports/dance/acting). Crafts.
	Learn best by –	Touching. Moving. Interacting with space. Processing knowledge through bodily sensations.
Interpersonal Learners	Like to –	Have lots of friends. Talk to people. Join groups.
	Are good at –	Understanding people. Leading others. Organising. Communicating.
	Learn best by –	Sharing. Comparing. Relating. Cooperating.
Intrapersonal Learners	Like to –	Work alone. Pursue own interests.
	Are good at –	Mediating conflicts. Understanding self. Focusing inward on feelings/dreams. Following instincts. Pursuing interests/goals.
	Learn best by –	Working alone. Individualised projects. Self-paced instruction. Having own space.
Naturalist Learners	Like to –	Observe things. Recognise things. Categorise things.
	Are good at –	Naming things around them. Finding connections between objects. Creating taxonomies and hierarchies.
	Learn best by –	Investigating. Observing. Linking. Analysing. Experimenting.

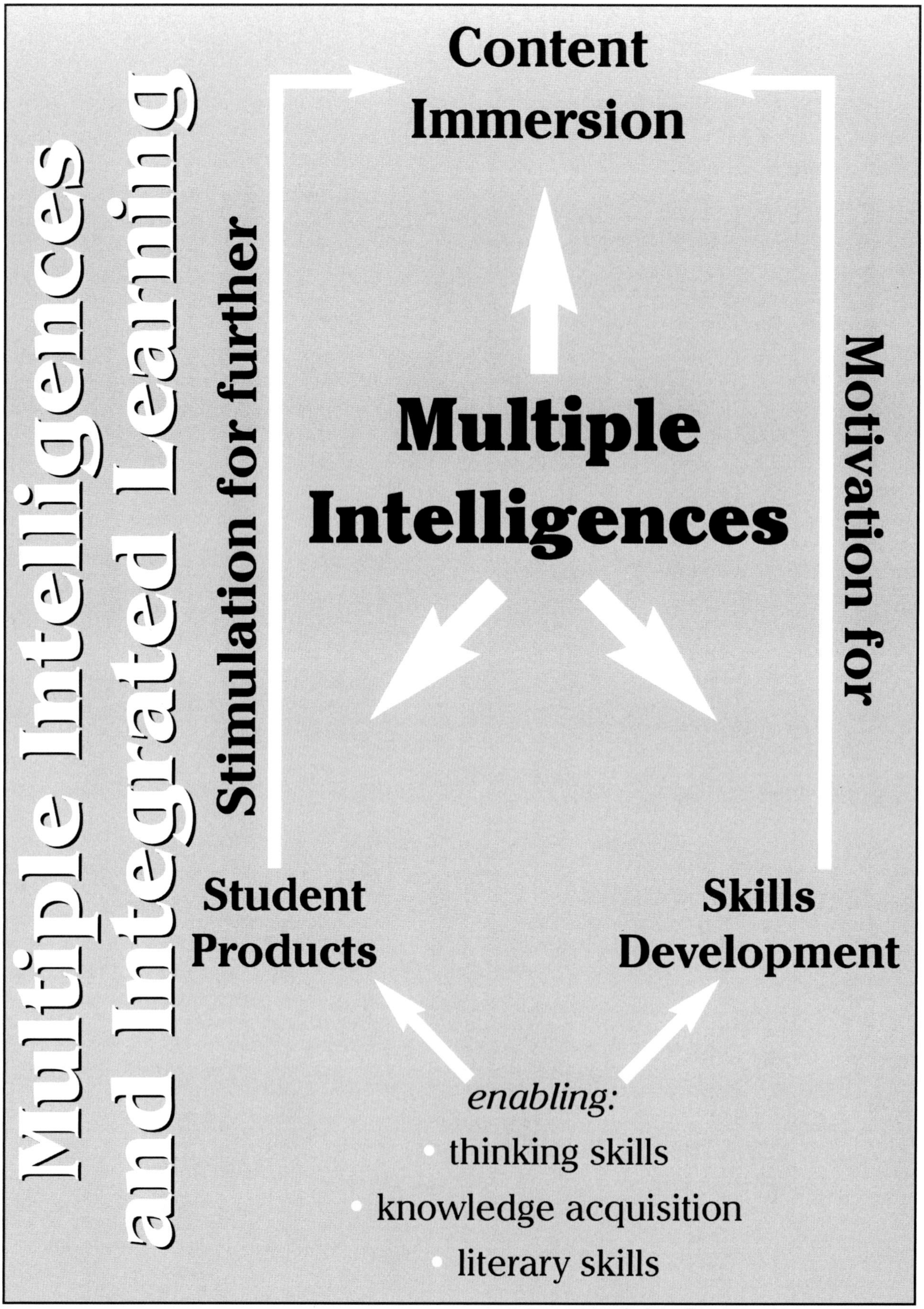

Content Immersion

Multiple Intelligences and Integrated Learning

Stimulation for further

Motivation for

Multiple Intelligences

Student Products

Skills Development

enabling:
- thinking skills
- knowledge acquisition
- literary skills

• Figure 4 – Multiple Intelligences and Integrated Learning

Examples of how Gardner's Multiple Intelligences may be applied appear on the pages that follow. These pages contain:

- a unit of work designed for primary students working on an underwater theme.

- a unit of work designed for primary students working on a theme of Australia – My home.

- a unit of work designed for middle years students working on a study of celebrations.

- a unit of work designed for middle years students working on a study of forest vegetation.

- an example of a Multiple Intelligence Activity Chart that contains a range of activities for students as they respond to a text.

- a blank planning proforma for teachers to use in developing their own units of work.

Section 2
Instructional
approaches to
tap into different
ways of knowing
and
understanding
the world.

Gardner's Multiple Intelligences
Theme: Under the Ocean Waves

Intelligence	Activity
Verbal/ Linguistic Intelligence	Create a word search of marine creatures. Do a PMI (Plus, Minus, Interesting) about a book that you have read about the sea. Write and publish a poem about life underwater.
Logical/ Mathematical Intelligence	Select three marine creatures. Show how they are similar and how they are different using a Venn Diagram. Show the relative speeds of a selection of marine creatures on a graph.
Visual/ Spatial Intelligence	Create a mind map showing what you already know about underwater life before you do research. Add to your mind map as you find more and more. Draw a colourful sea creature that uses camouflage as protection.
Bodily/ Kinaesthetic Intelligence	Create an accurate model of a sea creature out of clay. Mime the actions of various sea creatures and have classmates guess what you are.
Musical/ Rhythmical Intelligence	Create a sound effects tape to play as you present a poem about the sea to your class group. Create and teach a new round about the sea changing the words to Row, row, row your boat.
Interpersonal Intelligence	Work with a partner to write a story about a shipwreck that suddenly appeared at a beach that you were visiting. Discuss in groups ways that we may better preserve marine life in our seas and waterways.
Intrapersonal Intelligence	Read Scott O'Dell's Island of the Blue Dolphins. Write your own account of a lonely life on an island. What marine creature do you think you would prefer to be? Why did you choose that particular one?
Naturalist Intelligence	Collect pictures of sea shells and group them according to criteria that you select. Find out about, and try to remember the scientific names for, some marine life that may be found in waters near you.

Gardner's Multiple Intelligences
Theme: Australia – My Home

Years P-6

Intelligence	Activities
Verbal/ Linguistic Intelligence	Interview five adults about what it is that makes Australia a special place to live. Create a tourist brochure to attract people from Asia visiting Australia for the first time.
Logical/ Mathematical Intelligence	Graph rainfall and temperature information gathered over a month from each of the capital cities. Present a chart of the results of a survey on popular Australian pastimes.
Visual/ Spatial Intelligence	Try to order the states by area by visualising a map of Australia. Check your accuracy by checking in atlases and encyclopedias. Make a detailed clay model of Australia.
Bodily/ Kinaesthetic Intelligence	Shape a sculpture in plasticine that you would like to see in your capital city. Create a dance to accompany the National Anthem.
Musical/ Rhythmical Intelligence	Suggest music that would suit various attractions around Australia being showcased in a video for overseas tourists. Write and perform a song based on special features to be found in your local area.
Interpersonal Intelligence	Teach a 10 minute lesson to a group of classmates about a lesser known Australian animal. Work with a partner to develop a mock interview with a famous Australian from the past.
Intrapersonal Intelligence	Reflect on, and write a poem about a favourite location. What are your views about Australia as a republic? Write a diary telling your experiences as a new arrival to Australia during the late 1800s.
Naturalist Intelligence	Take some photographs that may showcase local attractions in a travel brochure for visitors to your area. Take rubbings of some of the flora native to your region. Classify them in categories of your choice.

Gardner's Multiple Intelligences
Theme: Celebrations

Years 7-9

Verbal/ Linguistic Intelligence	Prepare a speech that you may make at a family celebration. Write a newspaper article about a celebration held annually in your district. Do a recount of a festival or special event that you recently attended. Prepare some invitations for parents inviting them to a school celebration.
Logical/ Mathematical Intelligence	Use a Venn Diagram to compare and contrast celebrations in two or more cultures. Survey students – 'what do you celebrate?' Tabulate and graph results. Plan and cost a class celebration. Design wrapping paper based on geometric shapes symbolic of a celebration.
Visual/ Spatial Intelligence	Draw a Mind map of 'celebrations'. What has this picture to do with celebrations? Design a poster to advertise an upcoming event. Design a maze suitable for a child's birthday party.
Bodily/ Kinaesthetic Intelligence	Present a mime of a ritual or celebration that you have researched. Create a new dance suitable for a celebration of your choosing. Cook some dishes associated with a special event. Depict a celebration through a puppet that you have constructed.
Musical/ Rhythmical Intelligence	Change the words to a popular song to make it suitable to use at a celebration. Create a jingle to advertise a product for sale at Christmas time. Listen to music associated with celebrations around the world. Use musical instruments to create mood music for your next celebration.
Interpersonal Intelligence	With a partner, prepare and decorate invitations for a celebration you are planning. Use the BAR technique to improve on the design of your invitations. Share photographs of significant celebrations you have attended. Invite a religious leader to discuss the meaning behind some celebrations.
Intrapersonal Intelligence	Write a personal diary entry about a celebration you are looking forward to and why. Reflect on why a particular celebration is significant for some people. Collect poetry about celebrations that are meaningful to you. Are there some things that we should not celebrate?
Naturalist Intelligence	How might we recycle some things left over after a celebration? Visit some places of worship. Why are they situated where they are? How do some groups of people celebrate nature? Is physical location one of the more important elements in some celebrations?

Gardner's Multiple Intelligences
Theme: **Forest Vegetation**

Years 7-9

Intelligence		Activities
Verbal/ Linguistic Intelligence		Create a personal KWL chart (what you know, what you want to know, what you have learned) about forests. Brainstorm as many words about trees and forests as you can and add to the list throughout your study on forests.
Logical/ Mathematical Intelligence		Research and then draw maps to show the diminishing forests in a chosen area of the world over the past 100 years. Research and then graph the relative growth rates of some plants found in forests of different types.
Visual/ Spatial Intelligence		Create a forest display with a focus on issues of conservation. Prepare a detailed sketch of two very different rainforest plants.
Bodily/ Kinaesthetic Intelligence		Create charades to act out some of the words from your brainstormed list of words about forests. Make up suitable movements to 'Rainforest Music'.
Musical/ Rhythmical Intelligence		Add sound effects to *Jack and the Gum Tree* and then perform it for your class group. Research instruments made from forest trees and plants.
Interpersonal Intelligence		Debate the pros and cons concerning the logging and wood-chipping industry. Group brainstorm ways of preventing the destruction of forest vegetation.
Intrapersonal Intelligence		What do you consider to be the greatest threat to natural forests and bushlands today? What can you do to assist in protecting the surviving rainforests of the world? Write a personal reflection on this unit of work.
Naturalist Intelligence		Try to find out the scientific names of as many forest plants as you can. Write the common names on one set of cards and the scientific names on another. Play a game of concentration with a friend to help you to remember them correctly.

All Year Levels

Gardner's Multiple Intelligences
Responding to Reading Chart

Verbal/ Linguistic Intelligence	1.	Create a crossword, a spelling list and a wonder-word based on the story.
	2.	Summarise the story in your own words.
	3.	Write a diary for the main character including all major events.
Logical/ Mathematical Intelligence	1.	Show similarities and differences between two characters on a Venn Diagram.
	2.	Show major events in the story on a timeline.
	3.	Predict what might happen in a sequel to this story.
Visual/ Spatial Intelligence	1.	Mind Map the story using colour, pictures and words.
	2.	Create a storyboard of main events.
	3.	Draw a story map to show the setting for the story.
Bodily/ Kinaesthetic Intelligence	1.	Act out some of the words you created for your spelling list.
	2.	Mime a part of the story for others to guess.
	3.	Work with others to create a play depicting a major event.
Musical/ Rhythmical Intelligence	1.	Find suitable music to reflect the mood at various points in the story.
	2.	Add sound effects to the reading of a favourite part.
	3.	Write and perform a song based on the events in the story.
Interpersonal Intelligence	1.	Discuss the qualities of the main character. Agree on the 'Top 5' qualities.
	2.	Share the reading of a favourite part with a small group.
	3.	With a partner, change the ending by creating the next chapter of the book.
Intrapersonal Intelligence	1.	In what ways was the main character similar to yourself?
	2.	How did your feelings change as you read the story?
	3.	What was good, not so good and interesting about the story?
Naturalist Intelligence	1.	Did the setting have any effect on the story? Explain why you think so.
	2.	Find photographs of some of the natural features mentioned in the story.
	3.	Research about the climate for the region in which the story was set.

Gardner's Multiple Intelligences

Year(s)-

Theme:

Verbal/ Linguistic Intelligence	
Logical/ Mathematical Intelligence	
Visual/ Spatial Intelligence	
Bodily/ Kinaesthetic Intelligence	
Musical/ Rhythmical Intelligence	
Interpersonal Intelligence	
Intrapersonal Intelligence	
Naturalist Intelligence	

Instructional Approaches with a Focus on Critical, Creative or Caring Thinking

Few would argue the importance of developing the ability in young minds to be critical in their thinking and not to blindly accept what they see and hear. Students will require the ability to verify the validity of information, to be able to detect bias and to make decisions and judgements based on sound information or research.

Equally important will be the ability to be creative and not simply redo what others have done before them and to show a caring attitude towards themselves and towards others.

This section introduces four different planning models that encourage students to channel their thinking into essentially critical, creative or caring thinking modes.

Following the introduction to each model, practical examples are provided from different levels of schooling and from different areas of the curriculum.

The models to be discussed include:

- Taylor's Multiple Talent Model (Critical)

- Eberle's SCAMPER (Creative)

- Krathwohl's Affective Taxonomy (Caring)

- Lipman's Caring Thinking (Caring)

Some models can encourage students to channel their thinking into essentially critical, creative or caring thinking modes.

Section 3

Instructional approaches with a focus on critical thinking.

Taylor's Multiple Talent Model

Using Taylor's Multiple Talent Model as a planning framework will help develop the skills of critical thinking.

Instructional Approaches with a Focus on Critical Thinking

Planning units of work using Taylor's Multiple Talent Model as a framework will allow students to develop the skills of critical thinking as they investigate issues and work within topics and themes.

This section introduces Taylor's Multiple Talent Model (1963) as a planning tool for teachers who wish to have critical thinking as their focus for specific units of work. The model is equally adaptable for all levels of schooling.

Four of the six elements of the model encourage critical thought and reflection. These include:

Decision Making – considering alternatives, evaluating evidence and justifying a decision or stance on an issue.

Planning – deciding on pathways based on sound reasoning.

Forecasting – predicting future events and scenarios based on evidence, reasoning and logic.

Communication – using carefully constructed comparative, descriptive and clarifying language based on research, reasoning and evidence.

The other two elements of this model add some degree of balance by including:

Creativity – creating new ideas, new ways of looking at things or new products – having used some or all of the critical thinking processes outlined above.

Specific talents – planning to include the specific abilities of students, such as academic, musical, dramatic and artistic abilities.

Examples of how Taylor's Multiple Talent Model may be applied appear on the pages that follow.

These pages contain:

- a unit of work designed for primary students as they respond to a shared book experience.

- a unit of work designed for middle years students working on the theme of Christmas.

- a unit of work designed for secondary school science students involved in a study of energy use.

- a blank planning proforma for teachers to use in developing their own units of work.

Taylor's Multiple Talent Model
Text Study: Boss for a Week by Libby Handy

Years P-6

Category	Talents	Activities
Decision Making	- consider alternatives - evaluate possibilities - justify decisions	- Choose five rules that you would have in your home if you were boss for a week. - Select a picture from the book and give many reasons why you like this particular one.
Planning	- detail path to a specific outcome	- How would you show the results of a class survey on rules they thought they would like if they were boss for a week? - What convincing arguments would you use to persuade your teacher to let you be in charge of the class?
Forecasting	- predict events that may occur - looking at causes and effects of situations	*Think about and discuss:* - What you think it would be like to live in Caroline's house in the next week. - In what ways do you expect Caroline to change?
Creativity	- create new meanings - create new relationships - create new products or ideas	- Create a crossword or an acrostic poem based on words from the story. - Design a house fit for a 'boss' like Caroline.
Communication	- verbally - non-verbally	- Open to any page in the book and use the pictures to make up an entirely different version of what is happening. - What would be in Caroline's diary that week?
Academic **Dramatic** **Artistic** **Musical**	- fostering diverse special abilities	- Find meanings for words in the story which are unfamiliar to you. - Mime the story with a group of friends. - Design an interesting and different cover for the book. - How might you add music or sound effects to the story to make it even better?

Taylor's Multiple Talent Model
Theme: **Toys**

Years 7-9

Decision Making	- consider alternatives - evaluate possibilities - justify decisions	- Choose five toys that are popular with children of your age. List them in order of their suitability as Christmas presents. Tell why you selected this order. - Is Christmas time the best time of year? Why do you think so? - Have people lost the real spirit of Christmas? Explain.
Planning	- detail path to a specific outcome	- Who would you like to visit you during the Christmas holidays? Imagine they had permission to stay at your house. Plan a list of activities for a week that you could both enjoy. - What would you include on the menu for a class Christmas party?
Forecasting	- predict events that may occur - looking at causes and effects of situations	*Think about and discuss:* - What Christmas might be like in 100 years time. - What if everyone believed in Santa Claus? - What if Christmas was on a school day and not a holiday? - What if it snowed on Christmas day? - It was reported in the paper that Christmas had to be cancelled this year. Suggest five possible reasons for this.
Creativity	- create new meanings - create new relationships - create new products or ideas	- Create a novel way to encourage recycling of Christmas wrappings. - Use the BAR technique (bigger, add, replace) on Santa's sleigh to improve its efficiency, speed or looks. - Design a suit for Santa that is more appropriate for Australian weather conditions. - Create a new decoration for a Christmas tree.
Communication	- verbally - non-verbally	- Share the reading of a favourite Christmas story with a small group. - Pretend you are Santa and write his diary for the two weeks leading up to Christmas day. - What questions would you like to ask Santa? Try to list at least five questions.
Academic **Dramatic** **Artistic** **Musical**	- fostering diverse special abilities	- Use the alphabet key to generate 'Christmas' words. - Write and perform a play based on Christmas. - Design and construct a pop-up Christmas card. - Invent an dance, song, or mime about Christmas.

Taylor's Multiple Talent Model
Theme: Energy

Years 10-12

Decision Making	- consider alternatives - evaluate possibilities - justify decisions	- Choose what you consider to be the ideal solution to powering motor vehicles. Give 5 reasons for your choice. - List several advantages and disadvantages of different energy sources. - Would money be better spent developing a new power source or refining the use of an existing one? Do a P.M.I. on both viewpoints.
Planning	- detail path to a specific outcome	- Draw the features that you would like to see included in the design of an energy efficient house. - How can our school community assist in water conservation? - Plan ways the local government authority may save on energy consumption in the local area.
Forecasting	- predict events that may occur - looking at causes and effects of situations	- Predict a short term and a long term consequence should the price of fossil fuels be quadrupled next year. - What occupations would be affected should solar energy become a primary source of power? - How do you foresee savings from countries that become more energy efficient being spent? What effect would banning petrol engine cars from city centres have?
Creativity	- create new meanings - create new relationships - create new products or ideas	- Create a novel way to encourage recycling of household waste. - Use the BAR technique (bigger, add, replace) on a conventional form of transport to improve its efficiency. - Design a recycling machine/factory/process. - Make an advertising poster for a new energy saving product that you have invented.
Communication	- verbally - non-verbally	- Research and develop a video illustrating wasteful practices in energy use. - Plan an 'energy awareness' brochure on recycled paper. - Organise a debate on the topic 'The Sun is our Saviour – Solar energy as the key to future energy supplies'.
Academic Dramatic Artistic Musical	- fostering diverse special abilities	- Use the alphabet key to generate 'energy' words. - Write and perform a play based on energy. - Invent an energy dance, song, or mime. - Report on cost advantages (or otherwise) of using natural gas in households in preference to electricity. Collect real data to support your findings. - Construct a model of an energy efficient machine of your own making.

©2000 Hawker Brownlow Education #4552

Taylor's Multiple Talent Model

Year(s)-

Theme:

Decision Making	- consider alternatives - evaluate possibilities - justify decisions	-			
Planning	- detail path to a specific outcome	-			
Forecasting	- predict events that may occur - looking at causes and effects of situations	-			
Creativity	- create new meanings - create new relationships - create new products or ideas	-			
Communication	- verbally - non-verbally	-			
Academic **Dramatic** **Artistic** **Musical**	- fostering diverse special abilities	-			

Instructional Approaches with a Focus on Creative Thinking

Eberle (1991) describes SCAMPER as an acronym for a range of problem solving techniques that may be applied in any creative situation. It can be applied as a tool for creative production as students investigate everyday objects and seek to improve their design by considering the following:

S	Substitute	Substitute a person or object, or serve in a different way or role.
C	Combine	Bring together or unite Blend ideas, materials, situations.
A	Adapt	Adjust to suit another purpose or set of conditions.
M	Modify Magnify Minify	Modify attributes, frequency or size. Enlarge to make larger in form or quality. Reduce to make smaller, lighter, less frequent.
P	Put to another use	Use for an alternative purpose, in another situation or in a different way.
E	Eliminate	Remove or omit a quality, a part or the whole.
R	Reverse	Change order, adjust or create a new sequence, layout or scheme.

SCAMPER

SCAMPER can be seen as more than a design tool - it can also be used by teachers in developing creative questions for classroom instruction. Planning teaching and learning activities using SCAMPER provides teachers with a refreshing approach to writing motivating questions and will allow students to view a topic from some very different and often creative perspectives.

SCAMPER is particularly useful for the design of questions around a text, as the primary level examples that follow demonstrate.

The following pages contain:
- an example of how SCAMPER may be used in a design task
- questions designed for students as they respond to a text
- questions designed for students as they interact with a 'living book' on computer
- a blank planning proforma for teachers to use in developing their own units of work.

SCAMPER can be used by teachers in developing creative questions for classroom instruction.

SCAMPER

Years P-6

Topic: **Creating a Better Writing Instrument**

Substitute

· *Substitute a person or object, or serve in a different way or role*

Think about an everyday writing instrument such as a pen or biro. Brainstorm other uses for it.

Combine

· *Bring together or unite* · *Blend ideas, materials, situations*

Think about the attributes of a computer and see if this may help you to suggest improvements for a pen.

Adapt

· *Adjust to suit another purpose or set of conditions*

What might you need to adapt so that a pen may write in unusual places, eg underwater, upside down, on glass, etc?

Modify, Magnify, Minify

· *Modify attributes, frequency or size* · *Enlarge to make larger in form or quality* · *Reduce to make smaller, lighter, less frequent*

What could you make bigger on a pen to improve it?
What might you make smaller?

Put to another use

· *Use for an alternative purpose, in another situation or in a different way*

Imagine the pen to be twenty times bigger. Now suggest some alternative uses for it.

Eliminate

· *Remove or omit a quality, a part or the whole*

What could you take away all together to make it a more useful writing tool?

Reverse

· *Change order, adjust or create a new sequence, layout or scheme*

What could be reversed to make a pen a more useful instrument?

Topic: **Samantha Seagull's Sandals**

Years P-6

Substitute

• *Substitute a person or object, or serve in a different way or role*

Substitute the wise old crab with a playful sea horse.

Combine

• *Bring together or unite* • *Blend ideas, materials, situations*

How would the story change if Simon had wanted to be different also?

Adapt

• *Adjust to suit another purpose or set of conditions*

What else might Samantha use as she tries to be different?

Modify, Magnify, Minify

• *Modify attributes, frequency or size* • *Enlarge to make larger in form or quality* • *Reduce to make smaller, lighter, less frequent*

How would this story be different if Samantha was an albatross? What if she was only thirty centimetres tall?

Put to another use

• *Use for an alternative purpose, in another situation or in a different way*

What would have happened if the boots floated like a boat rather than sinking?

Eliminate

• *Remove or omit a quality, a part or the whole*

Retell the story, but take away the support from a friend like Simon.

Reverse

• *Change order, adjust or create a new sequence, layout or scheme*

What if Simon was the one who wanted to be different? How would he have expressed himself then?

SCAMPER

Topic: **Computers and Living Books**

Years 7-9   **Just Grandma and Me** by Mercer Mayer

Substitute

• *Substitute a person or object, or serve in a different way or role*

Substitute 'Grandpa' for 'Grandma' and tell how the story may be different.

Combine

• *Bring together or unite* • *Blend ideas, materials, situations*

Combine your knowledge of the solar system and ideas from the story. Retell the story set on another planet.

Adapt

• *Adjust to suit another purpose or set of conditions*

Adapt the setting of the story so that it now takes place in the mountains instead of the beach.

Modify, Magnify, Minify

• *Modify attributes, frequency or size* • *Enlarge to make larger in form or quality* • *Reduce to make smaller, lighter, less frequent*

When you mouse click items on the screen, some things come to life. Suggest something else that may be included, tell what it might do and suggest sounds that you could add.

Put to another use

• *Use for an alternative purpose, in another situation or in a different way*

Suggest other uses for flippers and goggles besides using them when swimming.

Eliminate

• *Remove or omit a quality, a part or the whole*

What part of the story could be left out? Why did you choose this part?

Reverse

• *Change order, adjust or create a new sequence, layout or scheme*

Imagine the story took place at night. Design a page set at the beach after dark or tell how the story may change.

SCAMPER

Topic: _____

Year(s)-

Substitute

· Substitute a person or object, or serve in a different way or role

Combine

· Bring together or unite · Blend ideas, materials, situations

Adapt

· Adjust to suit another purpose or set of conditions

Modify, Magnify, Minify

· Modify attributes, frequency or size · Enlarge to make larger in form or quality · Reduce to make smaller, lighter, less frequent

Put to another use

· Use for an alternative purpose, in another situation or in a different way

Eliminate

· Remove or omit a quality, a part or the whole

Reverse

· Change order, adjust or create a new sequence, layout or scheme

SCAMPER

Instructional Approaches with a Focus on Caring Thinking

Caring Thinking stems from the heart of the person - it is thinking with your heart, thinking about your personal values and thinking about others.

Introduced by Matthew Lipman, author of the Philosophy For Children Program, caring thinking can be seen to be the third of the three 'C's' that encapsulate the nature of complex thinking - the creative aspect, the critical aspect and the caring aspect.

Lipman identifies four major components of caring thinking.

Valuational Thinking

Valuing concrete things for their sensory or aesthetic appeal, rather than monitory worth. Appreciating nature, art or objects, acknowledging the intrinsic value or beauty in everything.

Valuing the abstract, eg. valuing attitudes, behaviours and personal qualities and the values of different societies.

Affective Thinking

The emotional response to a wrong doing by a person.

A clear understanding of right and wrong, and a strong moral sense of justice and genuine empathy.

Active Thinking

To passionately care about and be involved with a cause.

Using language, gestures, planning and/or action to support a cause or belief with a focus on what individuals may do about a circumstance or situation.

Caring thinking is thinking with the heart – thinking about your personal values and thinking about others.

Normative Thinking

To compare the actual situation with the ideal situation - it is about knowing the reality of the situation but having a vision or sense of idealism of how things should, or could, be on a local or global level.

Planning units of work around the four major elements of caring thinking encourages students to establish a sound value system from which to make sound and compassionate value judgements.

Examples of how Caring Thinking may be applied appear on the pages that follow. These pages contain activities designed for students in the primary years of schooling.

The activities include:

- two units of work designed for students as they respond to shared reading of a text

- a unit of work designed for students working on the theme of dinosaurs

- a unit of work designed for students accessing information via the internet in a study of contemporary authors

- a blank planning proforma for teachers to use in developing their own units of work.

Years P-6

Topic: **Responding to a text**
Princess Priscilla
by Stacy Apeitos and Beth Norling

CARING THINKING

Valuational Thinking

- *To clarify one's values & examine one's attitudes and behaviours*

– How do you think you would feel if you were told that you were too young to help out when you thought you were quite capable?

Affective Thinking

- *Attitudes and emotions around a clear understanding of right and wrong*

– Make up a list of things that children should be allowed to do and a list of things that children definitely should not be allowed to do.

Active Thinking

- *Focuses on the ability and willingness to support personal beliefs and values*

– Is it better to do things by yourself or with the assistance of others?

– Are there times when some things are better done alone?

Normative Thinking

- *Focuses on the alignment of the reality of a situation and the ideal situation*

– This story is fiction but maybe it has something to say to us about the way we choose to live our life.

– What do you think is the most important lesson to be learned from the story?

The Story of Linda and Clara

Years 7-9

Valuational Thinking

* *To clarify one's values & examine one's attitudes and behaviours*

– How did Linda react to being kicked by her friend?

– How would you have reacted in this situation?

Affective Thinking

* *Attitudes and emotions around a clear understanding of right and wrong*

– What decisions did Linda have to make after the kicking incident?

– What would be the consequences of each choice?

Active Thinking

* *Focuses on the ability and willingness to support personal beliefs and values*

– If you were Clara, what would you do to show that you are sorry?

– Should you tell friends when they hurt your feelings unknowingly?

Normative Thinking

* *Focuses on the alignment of the reality of a situation and the ideal situation*

– Could you ever really trust a friend who kicks you?

– What makes a great friend?

* *The Story of Linda and Clara* can be found in *Thinking Stories 1* by P. Cam
©1994 Hale & Iremonger

CARING THINKING

Topic: **Dinosaurs**

Years P-6

Activities to follow a viewing of the film *Jurassic Park*

CARING THINKING

Valuational Thinking

- *To clarify one's values & examine one's attitudes and behaviours*

– **Explain how you might have felt if you were Doctor Grant when he discovered that DNA had been used to recreate dinosaurs.**

Affective Thinking

- *Attitudes and emotions around a clear understanding of right and wrong*

– **'Dolly' - a sheep, was the first ever animal to be cloned. In what circumstances is the use of cloning acceptable? In what circumstances would it not be acceptable?**

Active Thinking

- *Focuses on the ability and willingness to support personal beliefs and values*

– **How important is it to protect animals in danger of extinction?**

– **What can you do to assist in preserving rare and endangered animals?**

Normative Thinking

- *Focuses on the alignment of the reality of a situation and the ideal situation*

– **Think about the destruction and chaos depicted in the film. How might this compare with what the world was really like when dinosaurs roamed the planet?**

Topic: # Author Study – Paul Jennings

Activities to follow up a visit to Internet site:
http://people.enternet.com.au/~jennings/

Years P-9

Valuational Thinking

• *To clarify one's values & examine one's attitudes
and behaviours*

– Paul Jennings has not forgotten the fears and feelings that he
had as a young boy.

– Explain a fear that you have and tell how it sometimes affects
the way you act.

Affective Thinking

• *Attitudes and emotions around a clear understanding
of right and wrong*

– Relate a story by Paul Jennings where the main character
faced the choice of telling the truth or not telling the truth.

– Did the character make the right decision? What makes you
think so?

Active Thinking

• *Focuses on the ability and willingness to support personal
beliefs and values*

– Is it important for an author to understand how readers might
be feeling?

– How might this assist the author to create more interesting
stories?

Normative Thinking

• *Focuses on the alignment of the reality of a situation
and the ideal situation*

– Some of Paul's stories deal with conflicts between characters.
Such stories may give us clues about the way we might choose
to live our life. Tell about an important lesson to be learnt
from one of Paul's stories that you have read.

CARING THINKING

Topic: _____

Year(s)-

CARING THINKING

Valuational Thinking

• *To clarify one's values & examine one's attitudes and behaviours*

Affective Thinking

• *Attitudes and emotions around a clear understanding of right and wrong*

Active Thinking

• *Focuses on the ability and willingness to support personal beliefs and values*

Normative Thinking

• *Focuses on the alignment of the reality of a situation and the ideal situation*

Section
Four

Integrated Instructional Approaches

As teachers become familiar with each of the instructional frameworks outlined in this book, they may choose to combine some of them as they plan and program across a broad range of thinking and feeling processes.

This section introduces three different integrated approaches that will assist in achieving a balanced program of activities for student instruction.

Following the introduction to each approach, practical examples are provided from different levels of schooling and from different areas of the curriculum.

The approaches to be discussed include:

- a combined Bloom's Taxonomy and Gardner's Multiple Intelligences framework

- a combined Bloom's Taxonomy and Krathwohl's Taxonomy framework

- the Divergent Thinking model.

Using an integrated approach can assist in achieving a balanced program of activities for student instruction.

Bloom's Taxonomy and Gardner's Multiple Intelligences

Integrating Bloom's Taxonomy and Gardner's Multiple Intelligences will see teachers planning and programming in a balanced fashion across the six levels of thinking as described in his taxonomy and also across the eight different ways of knowing and understanding the world as described by Gardner.

Examples of how the framework integrating Bloom's Taxonomy and Gardner's Multiple Intelligences may be applied appear on the pages that follow.

These pages contain:

- a unit of work designed for primary students working within a science topic on mini-beasts

- a unit of work designed for primary students working within a theme on Australian Aboriginal culture

- a unit of work[1] designed for middle years students working within a nautical theme of ships and shipwrecks

- a blank planning proforma for teachers to use in developing their own units of work.

[1] This unit of work demonstrates that it is not a requirement that activities are created for every box within the grid. However, by mapping activities in this way, the teacher can be mindful of areas not attended to in this unit of work, and may seek to include them in subsequent units. In this way a balance of activities is still achieved, but over a longer period of time.

Framework Integrating Bloom's Taxonomy and Gardner's Multiple Intelligences

Topic: Mini-Beasts

Years P-6

GARDNER'S MULTIPLE INTELLIGENCES

	Verbal/Linguistic	Logical/Mathematical	Visual/Spatial	Bodily/Kinaesthetic	Musical/Rhythmical	Interpersonal	Intrapersonal	Naturalist
Remembering	Do an A-Z of words about mini-beasts. Add to the list as you learn more about them.	Gather pictures of mini-beasts. How many different ways can you find to group them?	Make some space on a pin-up board to display pictures of mini-beasts that you find.	Mime how many different insects move.	Listen to the story of the Very Hungry Caterpillar. Clap the syllables of key words.	Select a spot around the school grounds to go to do a mini-beast safari with a group of friends.	Start a learning log about a mini-beast that you want to know more about. Add to it daily.	Record and talk about different types of spiders that you find around the school yard.
Understanding	How would you describe a fly to someone from outer space?	Draw the different stages of the life cycle of a butterfly.	Using materials found in the classroom, make a model of a mini-beast.	Role play a mini-beast as it undergoes metamorphosis.	Do all mini-beasts make noises? What body parts are used by some to make sound?	Work with a friend to find out more about the home of a particular mini-beast.	Research to find out why some insects like mosquitoes can rest on the surface of water without sinking.	Why do you think different spiders were found in different sorts of places?
Applying	Make up a 'What am I?' game for a mini-beast of your choosing.	Using materials found in the room, make up an obstacle course that would be challenging for an ant.	Use a picture of a mini-beast stuck on card to make a jigsaw.	Act out how a mini-beast of your choice protects itself from danger.	Make an audio tape of mini-beast noises.	Together with a friend, make a model of the usual home of the mini-beast that you researched earlier.	What insect is most like you? Why do you think so?	Use a magnifying glass to look closely at mini-beasts in the environment.
Analysing	What are some similarities and differences you can see in pictures of moths and butterflies?	Survey favourite insects in your class. Draw a picture graph of your findings.	Draw a diagram of a mini-beast and label each body part.	Make plasticine parts of many different mini-beasts.	Sort pictures of mini-beasts according to the noises they make.	Decide what made the home of the mini-beast you studied a good one. Do this activity with a partner.	Add names of mini-beasts to finish sentences like: As fast as – As small as – As deadly as –	What precautions should you take when searching for mini-beasts in the environment.
Evaluating	List the 5 things that you think are most important to remember when keeping a mini-beast in the classroom.	In your opinion, which insect is the most useful? Give many reasons for your selection.	Paint a poster showing your feelings about insect sprays.	Suggest five reasons why you think the design of your new mini-beast is a good one.	What do you think about the audio tape you made? What do you think makes it special or different?	Have a debate with a friend about whether a mini-beast is a pest or a friend to people. (e.g. spiders, flies, moths).	How would you feel if your were a grub about to turn into a butterfly? Explain your feelings.	Should mini-beast specimens be taken from the environment and kept in collections? Why do you think so?
Creating	How would the story The Very Hungry Caterpillar have been different if the story was about an ant instead of a caterpillar?	Write down some common ways that people protect themselves from insect bites. Now create a new or unusual method.	Design a new stamp with a mini-beast theme.	Use the plasticine parts to create a new mini-beast of your own design.	Create a title and cover design for the audio tape of mini-beast noises you made earlier.	Suggest some other places that would make a good home for the mini-beast that you studied. Do this activity with a partner.	Write a story about a day in your life as a – (name of a mini-beast).	Create a play about a mini-beast and how it has an important part to play in the balance of nature.

BLOOM'S TAXONOMY

Framework Integrating Bloom's Taxonomy and Gardner's Multiple Intelligences

Topic: Australian Aboriginals — Years P-6

GARDNER'S MULTIPLE INTELLIGENCES

	Verbal/Linguistic	Logical/Mathematical	Visual/Spatial	Bodily/Kinaesthetic	Musical/Rhythmical	Interpersonal	Intrapersonal	Naturalist
Remembering	For your assigned Aboriginal group, find their location on a map and describe the natural environment. Or Do an A-Z of words to do with Aboriginal studies.	Survey the class – how many students have thrown a boomerang, climbed Uluru, have an Aboriginal painting., etc. Graph the results.	Draw some Aboriginal tools and weapons and act out how they are used.		Listen to some music by an Aboriginal group or singer. Identify and name the instruments you hear.	With a partner, research and write a list of as many Aboriginal groups as you can find in South Australia.	Make a mind map of what you already know about Australian Aboriginals.	List medical purposes for different plants used by Aboriginal people.
Understanding	Write a 'Who Am I' / 'What am I' for: - An Aboriginal person - An Australian animal - Aboriginal tool/ weapon	Make a timeline to include significant events in the history of your assigned Aboriginal group.	In groups, discuss then draw what your assigned Aboriginal group's environment may have looked like before European settlement.	In groups, using appropriate music, mime/role play your understanding of how Aboriginal people may have felt about the first European settlement. Or Role play your group's understanding of European settler's reactions to discovering Aboriginals in Australia.		Aboriginal groups have places with special significance called sacred sites. Describe your own special place or significant site.		Find out what is in some plants that gives them healing properties.
Applying	Design an instruction booklet on how to throw a boomerang using a woomera.	Design a game for people to play and learn more about European settlement.	Assemble a collection of photographs, newspaper/ magazine cut-outs to highlight famous Aboriginals.	Using a puppet, act out a Dreaming story.	Use some natural objects to create sound patterns or tunes of your own.	With a partner or by yourself, write a set of instructions on how to use an Aboriginal tool used by a South Australian Aboriginal group.		Design and make an Aboriginal home or artifacts using natural materials.
Analysing	Design a questionnaire to use when we have our Aboriginal visitor. Write at least five open questions.	Use a Venn Diagram to compare Aboriginal life: - Before settlement - Just after settlement - In the 1990s.	Make a diorama of an Aboriginal campsite.	Handle some Aboriginal artifacts whilst blindfolded. How many can you guess correctly?	Group instruments used by various Aboriginal groups into categories.	With a partner, make a jigsaw puzzle of where different Aboriginal groups live in South Australia.	Write a biography of a famous Aboriginal. Focus on why they are famous.	List the attributes of a gum tree. Use SCUMPS - Size, Colour, Uses, Materials, Parts, Shape.
Evaluating	List many recommendations you would make for a group wishing to settle in a land belonging to another group.	What would be the good points and bad points about a long stay in a remote area?	Rank five pieces of Aboriginal art from most liked to least liked. Justify your ranking.	In groups, role play a different perspective on how European settlement in Australia could have been improved.	Listen to some music by an Aboriginal group or singers. Tell what message you think is contained in the song. Give reasons.	Debate in small groups: - Why Australia should become a Republic. - Why Australia needs a new flag.	How would you feel if a freeway was to be built through your home? Write an exposition to the government supporting or not supporting the proposal.	What can we learn about caring for the natural environment from the special relationship that Aboriginal groups share with the land?
Creating	Write your own story based on a Dreaming story.	Write an acrostic poem using the word – ABORIGINALITY	Design a CD cover for a new Australian record using Aboriginal Art techniques.	Create and compose a jingle/brochure/commercial advertising an Aboriginal tourist attraction.			Do a personal PMI on the topic of Australian Aboriginal Studies at the end of our unit of work.	Create a set of rules about caring for the land. Make up a poster to show your rules.

BLOOM'S TAXONOMY

Framework Integrating Bloom's Taxonomy and Gardner's Multiple Intelligences

Years 7-9

Theme: Ships and Shipwrecks

GARDNER'S MULTIPLE INTELLIGENCES

BLOOM'S TAXONOMY	Verbal/Linguistic	Logical/Mathematical	Visual/Spatial	Bodily/Kinaesthetic	Musical/Rhythmical	Interpersonal	Intrapersonal	Naturalist
Remembering	1. List the leisure activities that may take place on board an ocean liner. 2. List different types of ships and write a fact about each type.		Draw a sketch of a sailing ship and label 10 main parts, eg: – mainsail – mast – helm			Work with a partner to design a poster about lighthouses, flag messages, radar and sonar as safety measures for ships travelling the high seas.		
Understanding	Explain the various ways a ship may be powered.	Discuss silhouettes of ships with a partner and decide what type of ships they might be. How do you know? Record your findings.					Write a short essay explaining which 'mystery of the sea' is most interesting to you and why.	What are some naturally occurring things that may represent a danger for ocean-going ships? What makes them dangerous?
Applying	List 10 rules to ensure your safety on a boat.	As a captain of a ship, record your day at sea in your log book. Include details such as date, time, location, weather conditions, etc.		Mime 6 occupations to be found on an ocean liner.	Perform a piece of music with a nautical theme.	Teach the 'Port– Star' game to another group of students.		
Analysing	Use a Venn Diagram to compare and contrast a ship with an aeroplane and a train.	Group types of ships in some way and explain your grouping system.			Play a sample of music about boats or ships. Give details about the composer, instruments and where you might hear this type of music.	Work with a partner to come up with some questions to ask a Captain or Pirate about life on board a ship.	What type of ship is most like you? Explain your choice.	In what ways are ships like whales? In what ways are they different?
Evaluating	You are about to take a long ocean voyage in a handcrafted sailboat. Space is limited so you may only take 5 items. List what you will take and state why.			Work with a partner to create a television commercial. Your commercial must include a jingle to advertise a cruise on board an ocean liner. Present your work to the class.				Do you think that ocean liners contribute significantly to the pollution of our oceans? Give your reasons.
Creating	1. Create a shape poem about a ship of your own choosing. 2. Create two menus using Publisher. One menu for 1st Class passengers and one for the crew in the boiler room.		Improve the design of a passenger liner using the BAR Key. Design a postage stamp to commemorate a person, place or thing related to the sea.				Solve one of the many mysteries of the sea. Be prepared to share your ideas orally in a 3 minute storytelling session.	

Framework Integrating Bloom's Taxonomy and Gardner's Multiple Intelligences

Year(s)-

Theme:

	Verbal/Linguistic	Logical/Mathematical	Visual/Spatial	Bodily/Kinaesthetic	Musical/Rhythmical	Interpersonal	Intrapersonal	Naturalist
	GARDNER'S MULTIPLE INTELLIGENCES							
Remembering								
Understanding								
Applying								
Analysing								
Evaluating								
Creating								

BLOOM'S TAXONOMY

Bloom's Taxonomy of Cognitive Objectives
and Krathwohl's Taxonomy of Affective Objectives

This section introduces integrated approaches that will assist in achieving a balanced program of both thinking and feeling activities through the creation of learning activities around the integration of both Bloom's Taxonomy of Cognitive Objectives and Krathwohl's Taxonomy of Affective Objectives.

Practical examples are provided from different levels of schooling and from different areas of the curriculum.

These pages contain:

- a unit of work designed for primary students working within a theme of friendships

- a unit of work designed for middle years students working within the topic of gold

- a blank planning proforma for teachers to use in developing their own units of work.

Bloom's Taxonomy of Cognitive Objectives and Krathwohl's Taxonomy of Affective Objectives

Theme/Topic: Friendships

Years P-6

Bloom's Taxonomy of Cognitive Objectives

Taxonomy Level (Bloom's)	Focus Questions	Activities
Remember (Factual answers, recall and recognition)	Can you describe the facts or the situation?	Complete a 'Y' chart on friendship, telling what it looks like, sounds like and feels like.
Understand (Translating, interpreting, showing understanding)	Can you show that you understand the situation?	Make a chart showing the different things you do alone, with friends and with family members.
Apply (Using information gained in different, familiar situations)	Can you apply this information to another situation?	How might making a pen-friend be different from making other friends?
Analyse (Break into parts to examine more closely)	Can you break this information into parts, so that you may understand the structure?	Can you list some things that might make friendships change?
Evaluate (Judge, use criteria, rank, substantiate)	Can you form an opinion or make a judgement and give reasons for it?	Use the Directed Thinking strategy to discuss: It is best to only have one really close friend.
Create (Combine information and new situations to create new products, ideas, etc.)	Can you create some fresh ideas or new solutions?	Create a recipe for friendship. What are the main ingredients?

Krathwohl's Taxonomy of Affective Objectives

Taxonomy Level (Krathwohl's)	Focus Questions	Activities
Receiving Student displays awareness – listens, notices, observes	Can you identify with the situation?	Your friend has just let you borrow their favourite toy. How do you feel?
Responding Student wants to discuss or explain	Can you express how you feel or how others may feel?	Use some art media to express your feelings when you have a disagreement with a friend.
Valuing The student chooses a concept or behaviour that he/she believes is worthy	Can you make some choices or decisions about this situation?	What do you think it would take in order to be friends with someone very different from yourself?
Organising Student reviews, questions & arranges values into an ordered system or plan	Can you connect your values to the systems present in society?	How important are friendships to you? What other things may be just as important?
Characterising Student voices her/his beliefs and affirms his/her values	Can you state your beliefs and act accordingly?	What qualities do you need to be a perfect friend?

Bloom's Taxonomy of Cognitive Objectives and Krathwohl's Taxonomy of Affective Objectives

Theme/Topic: Gold

Years 7-9

Taxonomy Level (Bloom's)	Focus Questions	Activities	Taxonomy Level (Krathwohl's)	Focus Questions	Activities
Remember (Factual answers, recall and recognition)	Can you describe the facts or the situation?	Draw a timeline to represent the discovery of gold in Australia.	**Receiving** Student displays awareness – listens, notices, observes	Can you identify with the situation?	Tell how the miner in the story felt when he struck gold for the first time.
Understand (Translating, interpreting, showing understanding)	Can you show that you understand the situation?	Write a week's journal depicting life as a gold digger.	**Responding** Student wants to discuss or explain	Can you express how you feel or how others may feel?	Express how you feel after working all day.
Apply (Using information gained in different, familiar situations)	Can you apply this information to another situation?	Construct a 3-D model of a gold mining settlement.	**Valuing** The student chooses a concept or behaviour that he/she believes is worthy	Can you make some choices or decisions about this situation?	Design a suitable flag for gold miners. Explain your design.
Analyse (Break into parts to examine more closely)	Can you break this information into parts, so that you may understand the structure?	Write and perform a play based on gold-rush times. Consider period, costumes, speech, etc.			
Evaluate (Judge, use criteria, rank, substantiate)	Can you form an opinion or make a judgement and give reasons for it?	Discuss the impact of gold discovery on Australians then and now.	**Organising** Student reviews, questions & arranges values into an ordered system or plan	Can you connect your values to the systems present in society?	Determine and describe how miners may have felt when barricaded in the stockade.
Create (Combine information and new situations to create new products, ideas, etc.)	Can you create some fresh ideas or new solutions?	Using a series of key dates, create a history of gold 'rap' song.	**Characterising** Student voices her/his beliefs and affirms his/her values	Can you state your beliefs and act accordingly?	Compare our adventurous view of gold miners to the reality of being a gold miner in the 1800s.

Bloom's Taxonomy of Cognitive Objectives and Krathwohl's Taxonomy of Affective Objectives
Theme/Topic: Inventors and Inventions — Years 7-9

Bloom's (Cognitive)

Taxonomy Level (Bloom's)	Focus Questions	Activities
Remember (Factual answers, recall and recognition)	Can you describe the facts or the situation?	Draw a timeline to represent the milestones in the history of inventing.
Understand (Translating, interpreting, showing understanding)	Can you show that you understand the situation?	What makes some inventions especially interesting or accepted and others not so?
Apply (Using information gained in different, familiar situations)	Can you apply this information to another situation?	Construct a 3-D model of an invention of your choosing.
Analyse (Break into parts to examine more closely)	Can you break this information into parts, so that you may understand the structure?	Compare and contrast two inventions that have made life around the home easier.
Evaluate (Judge, use criteria, rank, substantiate)	Can you form an opinion or make a judgement and give reasons for it?	Discuss the changing impact of mobile phone use in Australia.
Create (Combine information and new situations to create new products, ideas, etc.)	Can you create some fresh ideas or new solutions?	Write and perform a play based on the life and times of a famous inventor.

Krathwohl's (Affective)

Taxonomy Level (Krathwohl's)	Focus Questions	Activities
Receiving Student displays awareness – listens, notices, observes	Can you identify with the situation?	Tell how someone may feel after creating their first invention.
Responding Student wants to discuss or explain	Can you express how you feel or how others may feel?	How would you feel at the launching ceremony for something you invented?
Valuing The student chooses a concept or behaviour that he/she believes is worthy	Can you make some choices or decisions about this situation?	Suggest ways you might encourage others to become inventors. Explain why you think your ideas may work.
Organising Student reviews, questions & arranges values into an ordered system or plan	Can you connect your values to the systems present in society?	Thomas Edison had many failures before inventing the light bulb. How would he have felt? How would you have felt?
Characterising Student voices her/his beliefs and affirms his/her values	Can you state your beliefs and act accordingly?	Compare the advantages and disadvantages of flying in aeroplanes. Do you feel the risk is worth taking? When is the risk too great?

Bloom's Taxonomy of Cognitive Objectives and Krathwohl's Taxonomy of Affective Objectives

Theme/Topic: _____

Year(s)– _____

Bloom's Taxonomy of Cognitive Objectives

Taxonomy Level (Bloom's)	Focus Questions	Activities
Remember (Factual answers, recall and recognition)	Can you describe the facts or the situation?	
Understand (Translating, interpreting, showing understanding)	Can you show that you understand the situation?	
Apply (Using information gained in different, familiar situations)	Can you apply this information to another situation?	
Analyse (Break into parts to examine more closely)	Can you break this information into parts, so that you may understand the structure?	
Evaluate (Judge, use criteria, rank, substantiate)	Can you form an opinion or make a judgement and give reasons for it?	
Create (Combine information and new situations to create new products, ideas, etc.)	Can you create some fresh ideas or new solutions?	

Krathwohl's Taxonomy of Affective Objectives

Taxonomy Level (Krathwohl's)	Focus Questions	Activities
Receiving Student displays awareness – listens, notices, observes	Can you identify with the situation?	
Responding Student wants to discuss or explain	Can you express how you feel or how others may feel?	
Valuing The student chooses a concept or behaviour that he/she believes is worthy	Can you make some choices or decisions about this situation?	
Organising Student reviews, questions & arranges values into an ordered system or plan	Can you connect your values to the systems present in society?	
Characterising Student voices her/his beliefs and affirms his/her values	Can you state your beliefs and act accordingly?	

©2000 Hawker Brownlow Education #4552

Divergent Thinking Model

Section 4

Integrated
Instructional
Approaches

The Divergent Thinking Model provides a concise and unifying approach to integrating important elements of thinking in both the cognitive and in the affective domain. The model presents seven different question types that teachers may use in structuring teaching and learning activities for students. The question types include:

Quantity Questions *such as*	List – How many – Give many examples of –	Which will stimulate **flexibility of thinking**
Change Questions *such as*	What is the short term and long term significance of – What would happen if –	Which will stimulate **creative thinking**
Prediction Questions *such as*	Suppose that– Tell the outcome of –	Which will stimulate **critical thinking**
Point of View Questions *such as*	Justify – Give your opinion –	Which will stimulate **affective thinking**
Personal Involvement Questions *such as*	What if you were – Imagine yourself as –	Which will stimulate **affective thinking**
Comparative Association Questions *such as*	Compare – Find similarities between –	Which will stimulate **analytical thinking**
Valuing Questions *such as*	Do you agree that – How do you feel about –	Which will stimulate **affective thinking**

The Divergent Thinking Model provides a unifying approach to integrating the elements of thinking.

Examples of how the Divergent Thinking Model may be applied appear on the pages that follow.

These pages contain activities for students in the primary years of schooling:

- a unit of work designed for students as they respond to a shared text

- a unit of work designed for students working in science on a theme about insects

- a unit of work designed for students working within a theme of Easter celebrations

- a unit of work designed for students working within a theme on Robots and Robotics

- a blank planning proforma for teachers to use in developing their own units of work.

Divergent Thinking Model   Years P-6
Topic: **Responding to a Text – Effie the Ant**

Question Type						
Quantity List... Give 5 examples of... How many...	How many ants were in the story? List all of the different animals that Effie spoke to.					
Change What if... What would happen if...	How would it be different if all of the ants spoke loudly?					
Prediction Suppose that... Tell the outcome of...	What would have happened if the caterpillar had stopped to speak to Effie? What if the elephant had been mean and nasty and didn't want to speak?					
Point of View Justify... Give your opinion...	If the other ants were telling the story, what would they say? If you were Effie, what would you have done? Why?					
Personal Involvement What if you were... Imagine yourself as...	Pretend that you are Effie. If no one wanted to talk to you, how would you feel? What could you do about the situation?					
Comparative Association Compare... Find similarities between...	In what ways are ants and elephants alike and how are they different? Find many similarities and differences.					
Valuing Do you agree that... How do you feel about...	In what circumstances would it be acceptable to talk loudly? Explain					

Divergent Thinking Model
Topic: Insects

Years P-6

Area of Study – Science

Question Type	
Quantity List... Give 5 examples of... How many...	Insects protect themselves from predators in many different ways. How many ways can you think of?
Change What if... What would happen if...	How would things change if insects were to suddenly disappear altogether?
Prediction Suppose that... Tell the outcome of...	What would happen if insect sprays were suddenly banned forever?
Point of View Justify... Give your opinion...	Some insects are thought of as pests. What do you think? Should we be trying hard to get rid of every last pesky insect? Why do you think so?
Personal Involvement What if you were... Imagine yourself as...	Write a poem describing your change from grub to butterfly.
Comparative Association Compare... Find similarities between...	How are people and insects the same? In what ways are they different?
Valuing Do you agree that... How do you feel about...	If there was a competition for the most useful insect in the world, which one do you think should win? Why? Which other insects should be in the running?

Years P-6

Divergent Thinking Model
Topic: Easter Theme

Question Type	
Quantity List... Give 5 examples of... How many...	List some places where you could hide Easter eggs in your bedroom that would make them difficult to find.
Change What if... What would happen if...	What if eggs were no longer given at Easter time? What if you could spend Easter in another country – where would you go?
Prediction Suppose that... Tell the outcome of...	How would Easter be different if it were celebrated in January? How would you spend Easter if it rained all day?
Point of View Justify... Give your opinion...	Tell about Easter from the point of view of a police officer, Easter Bunny, or a parent. Not everyone celebrates Easter – do some research about a celebration within a religion that does not celebrate Easter.
Personal Involvement What if you were... Imagine yourself as...	What does Easter mean to you? What does it mean to other members of your family?
Comparative Association Compare... Find similarities between...	How is Easter like: • a birthday? • Christmas? • just like any other holiday?
Valuing Do you agree that... How do you feel about...	Easter has both a religious and commercial side. Which do you feel is more important? Prepare an argument for a debate on the topic.

Years P-6

Divergent Thinking Model
Topic: Robots

Question Type	
Quantity List... Give 5 examples of... How many...	List as many places as you can where robots could be found.
Change What if... What would happen if...	How might your life change if you had a robot that could do all the jobs that you currently do around the house?
Prediction Suppose that... Tell the outcome of....	Suppose robots were outlawed forever. Would the world be a better place or would everyone be worse off? Why do you think so?
Point of View Justify... Give your opinion....	Do you think it would be a good idea to have a robot as a teacher? What disadvantages do you imagine?
Personal Involvement What if you were... Imagine yourself as....	Imagine yourself as a robot. Would you like to be without feelings? What advantages do you see for yourself as a robot?
Comparative Association Compare... Find similarities between...	In what ways are we similar and different to robots?
Valuing Do you agree that... How do you feel about...	It is suggested that the development of robot technology is responsible for some people being out of work. Do you agree that this may be true? What evidence can you find to support your view?

Divergent Thinking Model

Year(s)-

Topic: _____

Question Type						
Quantity List... Give 5 examples of... How many...						
Change What if... What would happen if...						
Prediction Suppose that... Tell the outcome of...						
Point of View Justify... Give your opinion...						
Personal Involvement What if you were... Imagine yourself as...						
Comparative Association Compare.... Find similarities between...						
Valuing Do you agree that... How do you feel about...						

Summary of Topics and Themes

Year Level

References

Resources listed here represent those that have been cited within the publication or have been influential in shaping the content of the book.

Anderson, L. (1999)   *A Revision of Bloom's Taxonomy of Educational Objectives,* paper presented to the Flinders University School of Education, Bedford Park, Sth Aust: Flinders University of SA. Feb. 1999

Bellanca, J. & Fogarty, R. (1989)   *Patterns for Thinking, Patterns for Transfer,* Victoria: Hawker Brownlow Education

Bellanca, J. & Fogarty, R. (1991)   *Blueprints for Thinking in the Cooperative Classroom,* Victoria: Hawker Brownlow Education

de Bono, E. (1992)   *Six Thinking Hats for Schools,* Books 1-4, Victoria: Hawker Brownlow Education

Buzan, T. (1995)   *The Mind Map Book,* London: BBC Books

Dalton, J. (1990)   *Adventures in Thinking,* South Melbourne: Thomas Nelson

Dickinson, et al. (1987)   *Brainstorming - Activities for Creative Thinking,* Sunnyvale, CA: Creative Publications

Eberle, B. (1991)   *SCAMPER – Games for Imagination Development,* Victoria: Hawker Brownlow Education

Fligor, M. (1993)   *Brainstorming - The Book of Topics,* Victoria: Hawker Brownlow Education

Kagan, S. & Kagan, M. (1998)   *Multiple Intelligences – The Complete MI Book,* San Clemente, CA: Kagan Cooperative Learning

Langrehr, J. (1996)   *Thinking Chips for Thinking Students,* Victoria: Hawker Brownlow Education

Lipman, M. (1994)   *Caring Thinking,* paper presented to the Sixth International Conference on Thinking, Massachusetts Inst. of Tech., Boston MA

Margulies, N. (1992)   *Mapping Inner Space,* Victoria: Hawker Brownlow Education

Parks, S. & Black, H. (1990)   *Organising Thinking - Graphic Organisers,* Books I & II, Victoria: Hawker Brownlow Education.

Pohl, M. (1997)   *Teaching Thinking in the Primary Years – A Whole School Approach,* Victoria: Hawker Brownlow Education

Ryan T. (1990)   *Thinker's Keys for Kids,* Woodridge, Qld: Logan West School Support Centre